CARPE JUGULUM

A Play

by Terry Pratchett

Adapted for the stage by

Stephen Briggs

SAMUEL FRENCH

samuelfrench.co.uk

FOR AMATEUR PRODUCTION ENQUIRIES

UNITED KINGDOM AND WORLD
EXCLUDING NORTH AMERICA
plays@samuelfrench.co.uk
020 7255 4302/01

Each title is subject to availability from Samuel French,
depending upon country of performance.

THINKING ABOUT PERFORMING A SHOW?

There are thousands of plays and musicals available to perform from Samuel French right now, and applying for a licence is easier and more affordable than you might think

From classic plays to brand new musicals, from monologues to epic dramas, there are shows for everyone.

Plays and musicals are protected by copyright law so if you want to perform them, the first thing you'll need is a licence. This simple process helps support the playwright by ensuring they get paid for their work, and means that you'll have the documents you need to stage the show in public.

Not all our shows are available to perform all the time, so it's important to check and apply for a licence before you start rehearsals or commit to doing the show.

LEARN MORE & FIND THOUSANDS OF SHOWS

Browse our full range of plays and musicals and find out more about how to license a show

www.samuelfrench.co.uk/perform

Talk to the friendly experts in our Licensing team for advice on choosing a show, and help with licensing

plays@samuelfrench.co.uk   020 7387 9373

Acting Editions

BORN TO PERFORM

Playscripts designed from the ground up to work the way you do in rehearsal, performance and study

---

Larger, clearer text for easier reading

Wider margins for notes

Performance features such as character and props lists, sound and lighting cues, and more

---

+ CHOOSE A SIZE AND STYLE TO SUIT YOU

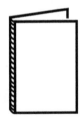

STANDARD EDITION

Our regular paperback book at our regular size

SPIRAL-BOUND EDITION

The same size as the Standard Edition, but with a sturdy, easy-to-fold, easy-to-hold spiral-bound spine

LARGE EDITION

A4 size and spiral bound, with larger text and a blank page for notes opposite every page of text. Perfect for technical and directing use

Other plays by TERRY PRATCHETT
published and licensed by Samuel French

Lords and Ladies

Making Money

FIND PERFECT PLAYS TO PERFORM AT
www.samuelfrench.co.uk/perform

ABOUT THE AUTHOR

Stephen says that, as all children know, the way you get into a fantasy world is by accident.... You go into the wardrobe, looking for somewhere to hide and – bingo. And that's how he found Discworld.

Stephen and Terry Pratchett played together on Discworld for 25 years and had a lot of fun along the way. In 1990 he had written to ask Terry if he could stage Wyrd Sisters. He had no idea it would go any further than one play (possibly two). But it did. He staged Wyrd Sisters in 1991. That was the first time anyone, anywhere in the world, had dramatised Terry's work. So far, he has adapted (and staged) twenty-two Pratchett plays. Most of these have now been published and they have been performed by amateur groups in more than 20 countries.

Stephen has also recorded many unabridged Pratchett novels for various UK and US audio publishers. He's won, and been nominated for, a number of industry awards. Despite those awards, regular listeners tell him it's easy to fall asleep while he's reading – not a good thing if you're listening in the car.

His written collaborations with Terry include the original Ankh-Morpork and Discworld Maps, the original series of Diaries, Nanny Ogg's Cookbook, The Discworld Companion (now called Turtle Recall) and The Wit & Wisdom of Discworld.

www.stephenbriggs.com

CARPE JUGULUM

First presented by the Studio Theatre Club at the Unicorn Theatre, Abingdon, on Tuesday 19th January 1999, with the following cast:

THE EXPERT/MORBIDIA	Victoria Martin
AGNES NITT	Sharon Stone
PERDITA X NITT	Claire Aston
COUNT DE MAGPYR	Stephen Briggs
COUNTESS DE MAGPYR	Kath Leighton
VLAD DE MAGPYR	Peter Laurence
LACRIMOSA DE MAGPYR	Catherine Long
IGOR	Trevor Collins
BIG JIM BEEF	John Kirchhoff
THE QUITE REVD MIGHTILY OATS	Colin Macnee
NANNY GYTHA OGG	Karen Hale
SHAWN OGG	Robin Allen
MAGRAT GARLICK	Tina Kempster
MILLIE CHILLUM	Sarah Young
VERENCE II	Tim Arnot
GRANNY ESMERELDA WEATHERWAX	Sue Hutchings
MRS SCORBIC	Lesley Young
SGT KRAPUT	David Weaver
PIOTR/CPL SVITZ	Graham Cook
JASON OGG	Keith Franklin
DEMONE	Rosie Everett
KRIMSON/SCRAPS	Claire Spittlehouse
CRYPTOPHER	Andy Allen
HANS	Simon Read
THE OLD COUNT	Mark Cowper

Directed by Stephen Briggs
Lighting and effects by Colin James
Sound by Phil Evans
Stage Manager: Mark Cowper

CHARACTERS

THE EXPERT, narrator

Witches and Family
AGNES NITT
PERDITA X NITT, *Agnes's alter ego*
NANNY GYTHA OGG
SHAWN OGG
JASON OGG
WAYNETTA OGG } *Nanny Ogg's children*
BERYL OGG
DUANE OGG
GRANNY ESMERELDA WEATHERWAX

Vampires and Followers
COUNT DE MAGPYR
COUNTESS DE MAGPYR
VLAD DE MAGPYR
LACRIMOSA DE MAGPYR
MORBIDIA
DEMONE
KRIMSON
CRYPTOPHER
THE OLD COUNT
IGOR, the de Magpyrs' servant
SCRAPS, his dog
SGT KRAPUT, soldier
CPL SVITZ, soldier

The Court
VERENCE II, King of Lancre
MAGRAT GARLICK, once a witch, now Queen of Lancre
MILLIE CHILLUM, her maid
THE QUITE REVD MIGHTILY OATS, an Omnian
MRS SCORBIC, palace cook

The Country

GERTRUDE
PIOTR
HANS
BESTIALITY CARTER
} *Villagers*

BIG JIM BEEF, border troll

DEATH

AUTHOR'S INTRODUCTION

An Awfully Big Adventure

Oxford's Studio Theatre Club were the first people ever to dramatise the Discworld. That was in 1991, with *Wyrd Sisters*.

We had a theatre that seats ninety people. We had a stage about the size of a pocket handkerchief with the wings of Tinkerbell. Put on a Discworld play? Simple...

A flat, circular world borne through space on the backs of four enormous elephants who themselves stand on the carapace of a cosmically large turtle? Nothing to it. A seven-foot skeleton with glowing blue eyes? No problem. A sixty-foot fire-breathing dragon? A cinch.

My drama club had already staged its own adaptations of other works: Monty Python's *Life of Brian* and *Holy Grail* – and Tom Sharpe's *Porterhouse Blue* and *Blott on the Landscape*. We were looking for something new when someone said, "Try Terry Pratchett – you'll like him".

So I ventured into the previously uncharted territory of the "Fantasy" section of the local bookstore. I read a Terry Pratchett book; I liked it. I read all of them. I wrote to Terry and asked if we could stage *Wyrd Sisters*. He said yes.

Wyrd Sisters sold out.

So did *Mort* the year after.

So did *Guards! Guards!*, *Men at Arms*, *Maskerade*, *Jingo* and *Carpe Jugulum* in the years after that. In fact, "sold out" is too modest a word. "Oversold very quickly so that by the time the local newspaper mentioned it was on we'd had to close the booking office" is nearer the mark.

My casts were all happy enough to read whichever book we were staging, and to read others in the canon, too. The books stand on their own, but some knowledge of the wider Discworld ethos helps when adapting the stories, and can help the actors with their characterisations.

The Discworld stories are remarkably flexible in their character requirements. *Mort* has been performed successfully with a cast of three (adding in an extra thrill for the audience, who knew that sooner or later a character would have to have a dialogue with themselves. But it turned out very well). On the other hand, there is plenty of scope for peasants, wizards, beggars, thieves and general rhubarb merchants if the director is lucky enough to have actors available.

I'd better add a note of caution here. There are a lot of small parts in the plays which nevertheless require good acting ability (as we say in the Studio Theatre Club: "There are no small parts, only small actors"). The character may have only four lines to say but one of them might well be the (potentially) funniest line in the play. Terry Pratchett is remarkably democratic in this respect. Spear-carriers, demons and even a humble doorknocker all get their moments of glory. Don't let them throw them away!

Terry writes very good dialogue. Not all authors do. But Terry, like Dickens, writes stuff which you can lift straight into your play. Although it was often necessary to combine several scenes from the book into one scene in the play, I tried to avoid changing the original Pratchett dialogue. After all, you perform an author's work because you like their style; as much of that style as possible should be evident in the play.

The important thing was to decide what was the basic plot: anything which didn't contribute to that was liable to be dropped in order to keep the play flowing. Favourite scenes, even favourite characters, had to be dumped.

I had to remember that not all the audience would be dyed-in-the-wool Pratchett fans. Some of them might just be normal theatre-goers who'd never read a fantasy novel in their whole lives, although I have to say that these now are a dwindling minority.

The books are episodic, and this can be a difficult concept to incorporate into a play. Set changes slow down the action. Any scene change that takes more than thirty seconds means you've lost the audience. Even ten-second changes, if repeated often enough, will lead to loss of interest.

The golden rule is – if you can do it without scenery, do it without scenery. It's a concept that has served radio drama very well (everyone knows that radio has the best scenery). And Shakespeare managed very well without it, too.

The plays do, however, call for some unusual props. Many of these were made by the cast and crew: a door with a hole for a talking, golden doorknocker, coronation mugs, large hourglasses for Death's house, sponge chips and pizzas, shadow puppets, archaic rifles, dragon-scorched books and Discworld newspapers ("Patrician Launches Victim's Charter"). Other, more specialised props were put "out to contract": Death's sword and scythe, an orang-utan, the City Watch badge, a Death of Rats, a Greebo and two swamp dragons (one an elaborate hand puppet and one with a fire-proof compartment in its bottom for a flight scene). Since the Studio Theatre Club started the trend in 1991, Terry and I have had many enquiries about staging the books – from as far afield as Finland, South Africa, Indonesia, Australia, Bermuda and the Czech Republic (as well as Sheffield, Aberdeen, Exeter and the Isle of Man).

So how did our productions actually go? We enjoyed them. Our audiences seemed to enjoy them (after all, some of them were prepared, year after year, to travel down to Abingdon in Oxfordshire from as far afield as Taunton, Newcastle-upon-Tyne, Ipswich, Basingstoke and...well, Oxford). Terry seemed to enjoy them, too. He said that many of our members looked as though they had been recruited straight off the streets of Ankh-Morpork. He said that several of them were born to play the "rude mechanicals" in Vitoller's troupe in *Wyrd Sisters*. He said that in his mind's eye the famous Ankh-Morpork City Watch *are* the players of the Studio Theatre Club.

I'm sure these were meant to be compliments.

CARPE JUGULUM

By the time we staged Carpe Jugulum in 1998, we knew that the Discworld plays were a winner.

As with all the adaptations, there were difficult choices about which scenes should be sacrificed to try to keep the play down to a reasonable running time. We had also realised that Abingdon's medieval Unicorn Theatre was a part of the package; it has its shortcomings, but its ambience contributed much to the success of the shows. This, for us, would particularly be the case as its oak beams and crumbling stone work would create a good backdrop for the Lancre and de Magpyr castles.

Carpe Jugulum had immediate appeal and we had fun watching the full range of vampire films to research the genre – everything from Bela Lugosi to Tom Cruise and every Dracula film, from Francis Ford Coppola's to Bart Simpson's.

This dramatisation (which runs for a fraction over two and a half hours) was written with the Unicorn Theatre's restrictions, and the number of players I expected to have available, in mind. Really complicated scenic effects were virtually impossible.

Basically, we had a bare stage with an onstage balcony at the back of the stage with a small curtained area beneath it. Anyone thinking of staging a Discworld play can be as imaginative as they like – call upon the might of Industrial Light & Magic, if it's within their budget. But *Carpe Jugulum* can be staged with only a relatively modest outlay on special effects and the notes that accompany the text are intended to be a guide for those, like us, with limited budgets. Bigger groups, with teams of experts on hand, can let their imaginations run wild!

In short, though, our experience and that of other groups is that it pays to work hard on getting the costumes and lighting right, and to keep the scenery to little more than, perhaps, a few changes of level. One group with some resourceful technophiles achieved magnificent "scenery" simply with sound effects and lighting ("dripping water" and rippling green light for a dungeon scene, for example). There's room for all sorts of ideas here. The Discworld, as it says in the books, is your mollusc.

The only change I have not made to this published script is to shorten the "gnarly ground" scene, cutting most of the "how they got to the cave" stuff. My cast would certainly have voted for that and it might shave some useful minutes off the running time. I am grateful to Irana Brown and to Terry Pratchett for that initial suggestion—and for encouraging me to bring Scraps back to life at the end of my production (a vote-winner with the audiences!).

Characterisation

Within the constraints of what is known and vital about each character, there is still room for flexibility of interpretation. With the main roles, though, you have to recognise that your audiences will expect them to look as much like the book descriptions as possible. *Carpe Jugulum* is, to an extent, easier in that many of the characters are not Discworld "regulars". Also, most drama clubs don't have a vast range from which to choose and it's the acting that's more important than the look of the player when it comes down to it! There is some character description in the script notes, but here is a little more detail about the main protagonists:

Granny Weatherwax
In the opinion of many, not least herself, the greatest witch on the Discworld.

She is nominally the village witch of Bad Ass in the kingdom of Lancre in the Ramtops (a mountainous and unforgiving area of the Disc). For practical purposes, however, she regards the whole kingdom and, indeed, anywhere else she happens to be as her rightful domain.

She lives in the woods outside the village in a traditional, much-repaired witch's cottage, with beehives and a patch of what might be medicinal plants. She owns a broomstick, but despite the best efforts of dwarf engineers everywhere, it cannot be started without a considerable amount of running up and down with it in gear.

Esmerelda ("Granny") Weatherwax is a formidable character with every necessary attribute for the classical "bad witch" – a quick temper, a competitive, selfish and ambitious nature, a sharp tongue, an unshakeable conviction of her own moral probity, and some considerable mental and occult powers.

Granny likes to look the part. She is tall and thin, with blue eyes and with long, fine, grey hair tied back in a severe bun. She wears sensible black, her skirt incorporates some serviceable pockets and her lace-up boots have complicated iron fixtures and toecaps like battering rams. She likes to wear several layers of clothing, including respectable flannelette petticoats. She wears a reinforced pointy hat, held in place by numerous hat-pins. She has perfect skin – a source of irritation; her complexion has resisted every one of her attempts to gain some warts.

Nanny Ogg
Gytha ("Nanny") Ogg is probably in her seventies. Her family arrangements are cosy but haphazard. She has been formally married three times. All three husbands have passed happily, if somewhat energetically, to their well-earned rest. She has fifteen living children.

Contrary to the rules of traditional witchcraft Nanny Ogg now lives in quite a modern cottage in the centre of Lancre, with up-to-date conveniences like a modem wash copper and a tin bath a mere garden's walk away on a nail at the back of the privy. The cottage is between those of her sons Shawn and Jason. She likes to have all her family around her in case of an emergency, such as when she needs a cup of tea or the floor washed.

Nanny's hair is a mass of white curls. She is a small, plump, attractive and good-natured woman, with a crinkled face, thighs that could crack coconuts and a large and experienced bosom. She smokes a pipe and, like Granny Weatherwax, she wears heavy, lace-up boots.

Magrat Garlick (Queen Magrat)

Once the youngest member (comparatively speaking) of the coven that Granny Weatherwax swears she has not got. Magrat is now Queen to Verence II, after a romance which was always on the point of foundering because the principals were invariably too embarrassed to speak to each other.

She was selected and trained by Goodie Whemper, a methodical and sympathetic witch with a rather greater regard for the written word than is common among the Lancre witches.

In a certain light, and from a carefully chosen angle, Magrat Garlick is not unattractive. Despite her tendency to squint when she's thinking. And her pointy nose, red from too much blowing. She is short, thin, decently plain, well-scrubbed and as flat-chested as an ironing-board with a couple of peas on it.

Magrat has an open mind. It is as open as a field, as open as the sky. No mind could be more open without special surgical implements. As a result, it fills up with all sorts of things. A lot of what she believes in has the word "folk" in it somewhere (folk wisdom, folk dance, folk song, folk medicine), as if "folk" were other than the mundane people she sees every day. She thinks it would be nice if people could just be a bit kinder.

She is, however, tougher and more practical than most people believe.

Agnes Nitt

Agnes is the new third member of the coven, having been recruited during the events of *Maskerade*. She is a small fat girl with a naturally rosy complexion; the sort of girl who would love to be a goth but was cut out by nature to be two goths. Easily swayed by her more imaginative friends, Agnes wears black, has a black hat with a veil, and even a black lace hanky, all this conspiring to give the effect of a small, low-flying thunderstorm. Despite her love of black, she has two shelves of soft toys. According to Nanny Ogg, who is seldom wrong in these matters, Agnes actually does have some useful magical talent. She walks with her feet turned out, has large hands and an amazing singing range and ability. Agnes is in two minds about everything. Inside every fat girl is a thin girl trying to get out; Agnes's thin girl is Perdita; Perdita X Nitt, who is everything that Agnes isn't. In *Carpe Jugulum* I've written Perdita as a part for a separate actress, seen only by us and Agnes.

Costumes

We played most of the characters in a form of Regency/early Georgian dress, though the men wore tights and buckle shoes instead of breeches. The male vampires wore Regency velvet coats and fancy waistcoats, with frilly shirts in the style of *Interview with the Vampire*. The females wore more traditional "Gothic" dresses with bat jewellery, etc. We put our Lacrimosa in a white dress trimmed with pink and a pink-lined grey cloak (to emphasize her rebellion against vampire traditions!)

We had our Scraps costume made specially for the show. He's available for hire from the Studio Theatre Club, PO Box 655, Oxford, OX4 3EU.

Panorama

Virtually none. We dressed the set in stage cobwebs, bats, mice and spiders. We had also pre-set the "You go, we belong dead" Frankenstein-type switch which Igor uses at the end to revive Scraps.

Apart from that, there were just the odd bits of furniture.

Special effects

Other little bits and pieces, not covered in the text, included:

Fangs

We knew we could spend up to £240 a pair having fangs made by a dentician, but we found some cheaper, glue-in fangs at Charles H Fox in London. Our vampires wore these for almost all rehearsals to get used to speaking clearly with them in. Our principal vampires (male and female) also wore fake nails.

The weather/explosions

We made heavy use of thunder, lightning and rain effects – as well as carefully chosen dark and threatening music under some of the dialogue – to boost the dark mood of the piece. As well as mains-powered, hired, theatrical flash pods for the bigger explosions, the Count also used a handheld theatrical flash device (purchasable from AJS Theatre Supplies in London) when commanding the weather.

ACT I

Scene One
A Bare Stage

At the back of the stage is a balcony with a curtained area beneath it.

When the play begins, the house lights dim. The stage is lit with an eerie light. Menacing music plays. Fog swirls across the stage; thunder rumbles and lightning flashes.

In the subdued light, a woman runs on. It seems she is being pursued. She looks this way and that, then moves to leave the stage.

A **VAMPIRE** *appears in the exit, blocking the woman's way.*

The woman turns and makes for another exit.

Another **VAMPIRE** *appears, blocking her path.*

The woman moves centre.

VAMPIRES *move in from each stage exit.*

One of the **VAMPIRES** *crosses to the woman and bites her on the neck. She screams and dies.*

The **VAMPIRES** *drag the woman offstage.*

One by one the **DE MAGPYRS** *enter and stand, silently watching the audience –* **VLAD**, *then* **LACRIMOSA**, *the* **COUNTESS** *and finally the* **COUNT**.

When they are all together, the **DE MAGPYRS** *advance on the audience.*

The music swells.

They stand for a moment at the front of the stage, observing the audience in the disinterested way one might look at food on a delicatessen counter when one is not actually desperately hungry, but knows one will be later! The music draws to a close; as it does so the **DE MAGPYRS** *snarl, turn and walk upstage, where they stand, awaiting introduction by* **THE EXPERT**.

Blackout.

THE EXPERT *enters.*

A followspot comes up on **THE EXPERT**.

THE EXPERT Hello, good evening and, er, welcome to Discworld. Discworld. A flat world, carried through space on the backs of four enormous elephants who themselves travel on the back of a cosmically huge turtle, the Great A'Tuin. On a world such as this, anything can happen.

The lights come up on the **VAMPIRES**.

Ah. *(He/she clears his/her throat)* Yes. These, ladies and gentlemen, are vampires. On Discworld, as elsewhere, there are many kinds of vampires. Two things have traditionally struck vampire researchers. One is: why do vampires have so much power?

The **VAMPIRES** *look smug.*

They're so easy to kill, they point out.

The **VAMPIRES** *react.*

Second: why are they so stupid?

Another reaction.

During the following, IGOR *enters, his back to the audience.*

I mean, wearing evening dress all the time is a bit of a give-away, their castles are full of things that can be used to defeat them – for goodness' sake! There're dozens of ways to despatch them, after all. And they spend the day in a coffin somewhere, guarded only by some elderly hunchback—

A spot comes up on IGOR. *He turns, as though surprised at finding himself on stage.*

—who doesn't look all that spry and should easily succumb to even quite a small mob.

IGOR *looks a little hurt.*

During the following, AGNES NITT *and* PERDITA *enter and stand upstage right.* PERDITA *hides behind* AGNES NITT.

These ones...are different. And they are on their way to the Kingdom of Lancre. At the invitation of the king. They're going to his daughter's naming ceremony.

The lights go out on the VAMPIRES *and* IGOR.

A spot comes up on AGNES NITT. PERDITA *is, as yet, not visible behind her.*

Also going to the ceremony is Agnes Nitt. Agnes is a witch. She was in two minds about going. Now she's in two minds about her pointy hat. Mind you, she's generally in two minds about everything. Inside every fat girl, they say, is a thin girl trying to get out. Agnes's thin girl is Perdita.

PERDITA *steps out from behind* AGNES NITT. *(**Note:** AGNES NITT is always accompanied by* PERDITA*)*

Only we can see Perdita. Agnes doesn't like Perdita. Perdita is vain, selfish and vicious. Perdita hates being trapped inside Agnes. She says Agnes is fat, pathetic and weak-willed.

AGNES NITT *pouts.*

During the following, **MAGRAT GARLICK** *enters and stands upstage left.*

Perdita thinks a witch's hat is a symbol of her authority. Agnes thinks—

AGNES NITT —I look like someone's dropped a liquorice-flavoured ice cream cone.

THE EXPERT Agnes is the third member of a three-witch coven along with Granny Weatherwax and Nanny Ogg. Of whom more later. She took over as third witch—

The lights cross-fade from the spot on **AGNES NITT** *to one on* **MAGRAT GARLICK,** *upstage left.*

—from Magrat Garlick. Now Queen Magrat of Lancre. Although she's given up the witching, Granny and Nanny are sort of proud that she has married the king. Mind you, although they might agree that she'd done the best thing for her, you couldn't help feeling that, compared with witchcraft, they considered marrying a king very much the second prize

MAGRAT *harrumphs crossly.*

Sorry, ma'am, but you know it's true.

The spot on **MAGRAT** *is cut.*

Agnes had to take over from Magrat because, well, there is a narrative symmetry about there needing to be three witches. The Maiden, the Mother and the Crone. With fifteen children, Nanny Ogg was the only runner in the race for the position of Mother. Magrat had been the Maiden, but what with marriage, and then...well, a baby...she was, well, disqualified and Agnes was recruited. Granny Weatherwax was never truly happy with having to be the Crone. But who else was there? *(He/she sighs)* Enough from me. For the time being. Let's get on with our play, shall we?

Blackout.

Scene Two
The Road to Lancre

On stage, downstage right, is **BIG JIM BEEF***, the border troll.*

We hear a coach and horses approach and stop.

The **COUNT**, **COUNTESS**, **VLAD** *and* **LACRIMOSA** *enter upstage left.*

COUNT Ah, gateway to the world. Well, gateway to Lancre, anyway.

VLAD And entirely undefended.

COUNT On the contrary, it has some extremely effective defences. At least, until now...

COUNTESS The witches should be on our side.

COUNT *She* soon will be. Interesting family. Uncle used to talk about her grandmother. The Weatherwax women have always had one foot in the shadows. It's in the blood. And most of their power comes from denying it. However, she will soon find out on which side her bread is buttered.

COUNTESS Or her gingerbread is gilded. That's the penalty for being a Weatherwax woman. When they get older, they start to hear the clang of the oven door.

VLAD I've heard she's tough, though. A very sharp mind.

LACRIMOSA Let's kill her!

COUNTESS Really, Lacci, dear, you can't kill everything!

LACRIMOSA *(sulkily)* I don't see why not. You're so unfair!

COUNTESS We let you drop rocks on the pixies, dear. Life can't all be fun.

COUNT No. I rather like the idea of her being...useful. And she always sees things in black and white. That's always a trap for the powerful. Oh yes, a mind like that is so easily led. *(He pulls his invitation from his pocket)* And this. Can you believe it? They invited us!

VLAD There are other witches.

COUNT Oh yes, we hope to meet them. They could be entertaining. Igor!

COUNTESS *(to VLAD)* Do you have a handkerchief, dear?

VLAD pulls out a hanky.

Give it to me please.

He does so. The COUNTESS wipes VLAD's chin with the hanky.

You have a few specks of blood. I told you to be more careful with that highwayman

The COUNTESS hands VLAD back his hanky.

COUNT Igor!

IGOR appears suddenly.

(startled) For goodness' sake, Igor, don't do that.

IGOR No, marthter.

COUNT Igor, why have we actually stopped here?

IGOR A troll'th in the way, marthter.

LACRIMOSA Run it down!

IGOR The old count wouldn't have told me to run it down. But then, he wath a gentleman.

BIG JIM BEEF waves. IGOR ambles across to him.

BIG JIM BEEF Evenin'. Dis isa bit embarrassin'. You know a pole?

IGOR Pole?

BIG JIM BEEF You know, long wooden fing...

IGOR Yeth? Well?

BIG JIM BEEF I'd like you to imagine, right, dat dere's a black and yellow striped one across dis road, yeh? Only we've only got der one and it's bein' used up on der Copperhead road tonight.

COUNT Get a move on, man! Run it down!!!

BIG JIM BEEF I could go and get it, if you like. But it wouldn't be here'til tomorrow, right? Or you could pretend it's here right now, an' I could pretend to lift it and dat'd be OK, right?

IGOR Do it, then.

BIG JIM BEEF Only first I gotta stamp somethin'. Shows you bin passed, officially.

IGOR What happenth if we jutht drive through?

BIG JIM BEEF Er – then I don't lift der pole.

IGOR looks confused by this metaphysical conundrum. He moves to the COUNT.

IGOR It'th a border check, marthter. We need to get thomething thtamped.

The COUNT hands IGOR the invitation. IGOR takes the invitation back to BIG JIM BEEF; he stamps it – with half a potato – and hands it back.

What'th thith? What'th thith thtupid mark?

BIG JIM BEEF I couldn't manage the official seal on half a spud. It's a duck. Not bad, eh? *(He mimes opening the barrier)* Now, look, this me liftin' der pole. Dat means you can go.

IGOR Marthter, we can go.

IGOR exits back to the coach.

COUNT Now, before we get back on the coach, I want you all to pay attention.

LACRIMOSA Father, we have done this before...

COUNT This point can't be hammered home enough. That is the Lancre River down there. Running water. We will cross running water. Your ancestors, although capable of undertaking journeys of hundreds of miles, nevertheless firmly believed they couldn't cross a stream. Hmmm? Cultural conditioning could be the death of us. Right? Let's go.

The DE MAGPYRS *exit.*

BIG JIM BEEF *watches them go.*

Blackout.

Scene Three
Lancre Castle

The royal reception is in full swing. Everyone who is anyone is there, with host, **KING VERENCE II**, *and guests chatting and servants (well,* **SHAWN OGG***) serving wine. The guests include* **THE EXPERT** *and* **AGNES NITT**.

NANNY OGG *bustles in, smoking a clay pipe. She moves to* **AGNES NITT**.

NANNY OGG Wotchagirl.

THE EXPERT *emerges from the crowd. While he/she speaks, the action on stage freezes.*

THE EXPERT Nanny Ogg is the head of a large family. She has fifteen children from three marriages. All three of her husbands passed happily, if energetically, to their well-earned rest. She lives in quite a modern house in the centre of Lancre, close to her family. She likes them to be near-at-hand in case of emergencies, such as wanting her floor scrubbed, or a cup of tea made. People often got the wrong idea about Nanny Ogg, and she took care to see that they did. One thing they often got wrong was the idea that she never thought further than the bottom of the glass. *(He/she rejoins the other guests)*

The action unfreezes.

AGNES NITT Lot of people here.

NANNY OGG Everyone got an invite. "Queen" Magrat was very gracious about that, I thought.

AGNES NITT Can't see Granny, though.

NANNY OGG She'll be somewhere, telling folks what to do.

AGNES NITT Haven't seen her around much at all, lately. Got something on her mind, I think.

NANNY OGG (*fiddling with her pipe*) You certainly notice things, don't you. Notice, notice, notice. We'll have to call you Miss Notice.

AGNES NITT   I certainly notice you fiddle with your pipe whenever you're thinking thoughts you don't like thinking.

NANNY OGG She has been a bit quiet though, you're right. Best left to it, though.

AGNES NITT   I thought she might be sulking about the priest they've got in to do the naming. King had one sent up from the Omnian Mission in Ohulan.

NANNY OGG He did what? An Omnian? Where is he?

AGNES NITT That's him.

> **THE QUITE REVEREND MIGHTILY OATS** *enters and looks around. He has a prominent boil on his nose and carries a book.*

> **THE EXPERT** *emerges from the crowd again.*

> *The action freezes.*

THE EXPERT The Quite Reverend Oats was in two minds about most things. Getting ready for the naming, he wasn't sure whether he should or should not use the mirror in his room at the castle. Mirrors had led to one of the church's many schisms, one side saying that mirrors encouraged vanity which was bad and the other side saying that, since they reflected the goodness of Om they were holy. Oats has not quite formed his own opinion, being by nature someone who tries to see both sides of every question. Oh, that's the Book of Om he's carrying. He knows most of it by heart, but he still likes to use it for guidance, by allowing it to fall open as Om commands...

> **OATS** *allows the book to fall open.*

OATS *(reading)* "...silence is an answer that begs three more questions. Seek and you will find, but first you should know what you seek." *(He shuts the book)* Oh, well.

THE EXPERT *rejoins the guests. The action unfreezes.* SHAWN OGG *takes* OATS *across to introduce him to* VERENCE.

NANNY OGG Omnians? Hah! Had a couple of them up here last year. Stuffed a leaflet under my door. It said "Repent!" Repent? Me? Cheek of it. I can't start repenting at my time of life, I'd never get anything done! Anyway, I ain't sorry for most of it. *(A new thought)* And they sets fire to people!

AGNES NITT That was a long time ago, Nanny...

NANNY OGG Hah! The leopard does not change his shorts, my girl! I'm going to have a word with young Verence. Just 'cos he's king's no reason for him to go round acting like royalty.

AGNES NITT I think it is, actually.

NANNY OGG Here – our Shawn!

SHAWN OGG *moves to* NANNY OGG.

SHAWN OGG Yes, Mum?

NANNY OGG You did deliver an invitation to Granny Weatherwax, didn't you?

SHAWN OGG Of course, Mum! And I dint just shove it under the door 'cos last year she give me an ear-bashing when the snails got that postcard. I wedged it in the hinges, good and tight.

NANNY OGG There's a good boy.

SHAWN OGG Erm...the queen would like a word with Miss Nitt, Mum.

AGNES NITT With me?

NANNY OGG It's a Royal Command, my girl. Off you go, then.

AGNES NITT *exits.*

Oh, and Shawn?

SHAWN OGG Yes, Mum?

NANNY OGG Be so kind as to let young Verence – His Majesty the King, I mean – let him know that Mrs Ogg would welcome the grace of his presence over here. Chop, chop.

SHAWN OGG But I can't say tha... Yes, Mum. *(He scuttles over to* **VERENCE***)*

The lights cross-fade to:

Scene Four
The Queen's Chamber

This scene takes place on the balcony.

MAGRAT GARLICK *is on stage, with the royal crib and the baby.*

MILLIE CHILLUM *enters and bobs a curtsy.*

MILLIE CHILLUM Miss Agnes Nitt, your majesty.

MILLIE *bobs again and exits.*

AGNES NITT *enters and bobs an uncertain curtsy.*

MAGRAT GARLICK Oh, hello, Agnes. You don't have to bob, you know. Millie does it all the time. Makes me quite sea-sick. Anyway, witches are supposed to bow. I just wanted a little talk. It's a bit... Look, I'm really very happy but, well... Millie's nice but she agrees with me all the time and Nanny and Granny still treat me as if I wasn't, well, you know, queen and everything – not that I want to be treated as queen all the time but, well, you know, I want them to know I'm queen but not treat me as one, if you know what I mean...

AGNES NITT I think so.

MAGRAT GARLICK Actually, Nanny's not too bad, but when Granny looks at me you can see her thinking "Oh, there's Magrat. Make the tea, Magrat". One day I swear I'll make a very cutting remark.

AGNES NITT I know what you mean.

MAGRAT GARLICK It's like they think this is some sort of hobby, and I'll get it out of my system and go back to witching. Is Granny here, yet?

AGNES NITT Haven't seen her.

MAGRAT GARLICK Ah, she'll be waiting for the right dramatic moment. Actually, no, not waiting. I mean, if it was you or me, we'd be hanging around in the hall or something, but she just walks in and it's the right time.

AGNES NITT She says you make your own time.

MAGRAT GARLICK Yes. But you say she's not here, yet? It was the first card we did! Verence got them to put on extra gold leaf. *(She sighs)* How are you at making tea?

AGNES NITT They always complain.

MAGRAT *nods.*

It's not as if they even give me tea money.

MAGRAT GARLICK It's not worth baking biscuits, either. I used to spend hours. You might just as well get them from the shop.

A pause.

She must have got the invitation, mustn't she?

AGNES NITT Shawn says he delivered it. And she probably said: "I can't be havin' with that at my time of life. I've never bin one to put meself forward. No one could ever say that".

MAGRAT GARLICK Gosh, that's clever. I even wrote a bit underneath asking her to be godmother. She's always secretly wanted to be one.

AGNES NITT That's something to wish on a child!

MAGRAT GARLICK Well, if it was a choice of wishing a child health, wealth or Granny Weatherwax on her side, I know which I'd choose. She'll never be beaten, you know? You wait til you see her in a tight corner. She's got that way of – putting part of herself somewhere safe. It's as if she gives a part of herself to someone else to keep hidden for a while. It's like that Borrowing she does.

THE EXPERT *enters; a spot comes up on him/her.*

THE EXPERT When there was nothing much else to occupy her time, Granny Weatherwax sent her mind Borrowing, letting it ride piggyback in the heads of other creatures. Seeing the world through the eyes of a badger, or a pigeon, or whatever. This practice meant, amongst other things, that Lancre people were less inclined to casual cruelty to animals on the basis that the rat you throw a brick at today may well turn out to be the witch you need to cure your toothache tomorrow. It also meant that people calling on her unexpectedly would find her stretched out apparently cold and lifeless, heart and pulse barely beating. To save embarrassment, she used to hold, in blue fingers, a little card. *(He/she holds up a card which reads: "I ATE'NT DEAD")*

The spotlight goes out.

MAGRAT GARLICK It's like those magicians in Howondaland who keep their heart in a jar somewhere, for safety, so they can't be killed.

AGNES NITT Wouldn't have to be a very big jar.

MAGRAT GARLICK That's not very kind.

AGNES NITT What name are you giving the baby?

MAGRAT GARLICK You'll have to wait and see.

The lights cross-fade back to:

Scene Five
Lancre Castle: The Party

The party is more or less as we left it, except that the
DE MAGPYRS *are now on stage, observing the guests.*

VERENCE *approaches* **NANNY OGG.**

NANNY OGG Ah, your majesty. Now look, I can't be havin' with Omnians doin'the namin', sire.

VERENCE With respect, Nanny, that really is a matter for the king to decide...

NANNY OGG They set fire to people! Witches!

VERENCE That was some time ago. They are much more tolerant, now, I understand...

NANNY OGG They say everyone starts out bad and only gets good by believin' in Om, which is frankly dam' nonsense. I mean. Look at your little girl – what's her name goin'to be...?

VERENCE Everyone will know soon enough, Nanny.

NANNY OGG Hah. Well, look, the worst she could put her hand up to would be a few sleepless nights and some grubby nappies. That's hardly sinful, to my mind.

VERENCE I think you're taking it too much to heart.

NANNY OGG Granny Weatherwax won't like it!

VERENCE Granny Weatherwax isn't king, Nanny. The world is changing. There is a new order. This is no longer a time when little kingdoms like ours need only worry about little concerns. We're part of a big world. New powers are emerging and we have to remain on good terms with them. That includes Omnia. I'm sure we'll not regret it.

The **COUNT,** *behind* **VERENCE,** *makes a gesture, summoning him.*

Excuse me. *(He moves across to the* **COUNT***)*

The COUNT *silently introduces his family to* VERENCE *under the following dialogue.*

AGNES NITT *and* MILLIE CHILLUM *enter in a rush and move straight to* NANNY OGG.

NANNY OGG Sometimes I think the weight of that dam' crown is turning Verence's head.

AGNES NITT Magrat says "Is Granny Weatherwax coming or not?"

NANNY OGG She'll be here.

MILLIE CHILLUM Only, well, the queen says we'd better not hold things up and so, er, will you be godmother, Mrs Ogg?

NANNY OGG Tell you what. I'll come and sort of stand in until Granny gets here, shall I? You tell her majesty that.

MILLIE *bobs and exits.*

NANNY *and* AGNES NITT *move to* OATS.

OATS Good, um, evening. You must be some of these witches I've heard so much about.

NANNY OGG Hah.

OATS I am the...aah. *(He pinches the bridge of his nose to prevent a sneeze)* Sorry, the mountain air doesn't agree with me. I am the Quite Reverend Mightily Oats.

AGNES NITT Mightily?

OATS Well, it's really "Mightily-Praiseworthy-Are-Ye-Who-Exalteth-Om" Oats. It's much shorter in Omnian, of course.

NANNY OGG And we'll have none of your heathen ways, my good man. No sloshing oil or water or sand around or cutting any bits off. I'll be standing behind you with a pointy stick.

AGNES NITT What's got into you? That's the way Granny would act.

PERDITA Perhaps she thinks she's got to act that way because the old bat's not here!

OATS And what is your role, er, ma'am?

NANNY OGG I'm the godmother!

OATS Er – which god?

AGNES NITT It's an old Lancre word. Means "good mother" or somesuch.

MAGRAT and MILLIE enter with the baby.

VERENCE moves to MAGRAT and MILLIE and the royal party assemble for the naming. The group comprises AGNES NITT, OATS and (slightly behind him, pointy stick at the ready) NANNY OGG.

MAGRAT gives the baby to OATS.

VERENCE Please begin, reverend.

OATS I, um, did have a suitable homily on the subject of hope for the... *(He jerks forward slightly, in the manner of one prodded from behind with a sharp stick)* But alas, I fear we have no time. Hrrm. We are gathered here, in the sight of... *(Another prod from the stick)* um – one another...

VERENCE Are you all right, reverend?

OATS Oh yes, sire. Never better. And therefore I name thee – er... *(He hands the baby to MILLIE, removes his hat and consults a piece of paper inside it. He replaces the hat and takes the baby again)* I name you: Esmerelda Margaret Note Spelling of Lancre!

MAGRAT GARLICK
AGNES NITT } *(together)* Note spelling?

NANNY OGG Esmerelda?

The action freezes and THE EXPERT steps out of the crowd. Behind THE EXPERT, the onstage actors withdraw slightly to the sides.

The onstage curtains open to reveal **GRANNY WEATHERWAX** *in her cottage. The lights come up on her. She sits staring fixedly ahead.*

THE EXPERT You'll recall young Shawn Ogg confirming that he had delivered an invitation to Granny Weatherwax, the Discworld's most powerful witch. But an invitation delivered is not the same as an invitation received and, even in Lancre, things do get lost in the mail. Granny Weatherwax has spent a lifetime serving and terrorising the community. Never looked for any reward. And that's part of the problem.

THE EXPERT *rejoins the crowd.*

GRANNY WEATHERWAX They didn't ask me. Didn't even bloody ask me. It's a sign. I suppose I've expected it, sooner or later. Too much to expect gratitude. The reward for toil is always more toil. If you dig the best ditches, they give you a bigger shovel. And I got this. Bare walls, bare floor. This cold cottage. Didn't bloody ask me. All I've done for them and never asked anything in return. Trouble with that is, sometimes you get nothing. I've always tried to face the light. Difficult choices sometimes. And the harder you stare into the light, the stronger the temptation is to turn and see the long, rich, dark shadow, streaming away behind you... They didn't ask me. Well, they can bloody well do without me!

The lights go out on the cottage scene and the curtains close. The castle guests return to the positions they held before the cottage scene.

MAGRAT GARLICK Note Spelling?

NANNY OGG Definitely a bit tricky. Esmerelda, now that's a good one. Gytha would've been good, too, but can't argue with Esmerelda...

AGNES NITT Definitely.

NANNY OGG But you know kids. They'll be calling her Spelly.

MAGRAT GARLICK I didn't expect anyone to say "Note Spelling" – I just wanted to make sure she didn't end up being called Magrat, like me.

VERENCE We can change it, can't we? Where's the royal historian?

SHAWN OGG *(with a polite cough)* Well it's not actually Thursday evening, sire, and I'd have to go and fetch the proper hat...

VERENCE Can we change it or not, man?

SHAWN OGG Er...it has been said, sire. At the official time.

NANNY OGG No, you can't change it. Look at old Moocow Poorchick over in Slice, for one.

VERENCE *looks confused.*

MAGRAT GARLICK His full name is James "What-the-Hell's-That-Cow-Doing-In-Here?" Poorchick. And if my mother had been sensible enough to tell Father Perdore my name instead of writing it down, life would've been a whole lot different. *(She glances nervously at* **VERENCE***)* Probably worse, of course.

VERENCE So I've got to take Esmerelda out to her people and tell them one of her names is Note Spelling?

NANNY OGG Well, we did have a king called My Gods He's Heavy the First.

VERENCE Oh well. Let me have her.

OATS *whimpers slightly.*

And someone get this man a drink.

SHAWN OGG *exits to fetch* **OATS** *a drink.*

VERENCE *exits with the baby, to show it to his subjects.*

There is crowd noise off.

OATS *(to the room in general)* I'm really terribly sorry.

NANNY OGG But where's Esme? She'd know about this, you mark my words. A princess named after her? She'll be crowing about it for months. I'm going to see what's going on.

NANNY OGG *exits.*

SHAWN OGG *enters with a drink for* **OATS.**

AGNES NITT *takes the drink.*

SHAWN OGG *exits.*

AGNES NITT *(to* **OATS***)* Here, drink this.

OATS I don't drink alcohol.

AGNES NITT Well, perhaps you should have a sit down and pull yourself together. There's going to be dancing later on.

OATS Oh, I don't dance. Dancing is a snare to entrap the weak-willed...

AGNES NITT Well, there's the ox roast outside...

OATS We only eat fish this month. The prophet Brutha eschewed meat when he was wandering in the desert.

AGNES NITT And what meat is there? In a desert? Doesn't sound like much of a sacrifice to me.

OATS Well, I'd need to check with Brother Melchio on that one, um... Er – perhaps I'll see if they have any squash. Non-citrus, of course, on a Wednesday.

AGNES NITT Of course.

OATS *exits.*

VLAD *moves across to* **AGNES NITT.**

VLAD Who is that strange person?

AGNES NITT Er – sorry?

PERDITA Hey. Now he's cool!

VLAD You can practically smell him. He looks like a bedraggled crow.

PERDITA Say something to him, dummy.

AGNES NITT Wstfgl?

VLAD I beg your pardon?

AGNES NITT He does look as if he's about to flap away, doesn't he?

PERDITA Please. Don't giggle.

AGNES NITT *giggles.*

VLAD Can I get you a drink, Miss Nitt?

AGNES NITT Er – white wine?

VLAD The red is much more – colourful.

PERDITA Ask him his name! Find out where he's from!

AGNES NITT *(to* **PERDITA***)* No. That would be forward of me.

PERDITA You were built forward!!!

VLAD Please let me introduce myself. I'm Vlad. My sister and I have—

SHAWN OGG *enters and moves to* **AGNES NITT***'s side.*

SHAWN OGG Excuse me?

AGNES NITT Yes, Shawn?

PERDITA Drop dead, Shawn Ogg!

SHAWN OGG I'm having to tell everyone that the king would welcome their attendance at the ox roast.

The crowd, including the **DE MAGPYRS***, move towards the exit.*

VLAD Sounds delicious. Might I escort you, Miss Nitt?

SHAWN OGG Er – Mum says can she have a word. It's important, she says.

NANNY OGG *enters and stands upstage.*

PERDITA It always is.

AGNES NITT *(to* VLAD*)* Excuse me. I have to go and help an old lady.

VLAD I'm sure we'll meet again.

Everyone except NANNY OGG, AGNES NITT *and* PERDITA *exit.*

AGNES NITT *(moving to* NANNY*)* Yes, Nanny? What is so important?

NANNY OGG Do you know whose carriage I saw outside? Some bigwig from Überwald's, that's whose. They're all mad scientists, vampires and werewolves over there. We'll all be murdered in one another's beds!

IGOR *enters and crosses the stage, carrying a couple of large boxes.*

Er—'scuse me, Igor.

IGOR *puts down the boxes and moves to* NANNY OGG.

IGOR What made you think my name wath Igor? You think everyone from Überwald ith called Igor, don't you? I could have any one of thouthandth of nameth, woman.

NANNY OGG So what is your name?

IGOR Igor. But it might not have been!

NANNY OGG I used to know an Igor from Überwald. Walked with a limp. One eye a bit higher than the other. Had the same – manner – of speaking.

IGOR Thoundth like my Uncle Igor. He worked for the mad doctor at Blitnitz, n' he wath a proper mad doctor, not like the mad doctorth you get thethe dayth. Don't get the right calibre of thervanth thethe dayth, either. When my Uncle Igor went for a geniuth'th brain, he got a geniuth'th brain.

He didn't drop the jar and thubthitute a brain out of the "Really Inthane" jar. No thir – er, ma'am.

NANNY OGG I think I've heard of him. Didn't he used to stitch folk together out of dead parts?

AGNES NITT No! Really?

NANNY *presses her boot on to* **AGNES NITT***'s toe.*

Ow!

NANNY OGG Nothing wrong with that. I call it prudent. So, is that your master's coach outside, then, Igor?

IGOR Call them marthterth? Huh! Now the old count, he wath a gentleman of the old thcool. He alwayth wore evening dreth. None of thith fanthy waithcoat thtuff! You know what they done?

NANNY OGG Do tell.

IGOR They only oiled the hingeth! Thome of thothe thkweakth had taken thenturieth to get right! But oh, no, it'th "Igor, thweep away thothe thpider'th webth, get thome proper candleth in". It'th not right. People exthpect thertain thtandardth.

NANNY OGG You got to get the details right, I always say. If your coach breaks down near the castle, you expect creaky doors and dribbling candles—

IGOR Exactly.

NANNY OGG —a room with a balcony outside and billowy curtains—

IGOR Yeth!

NANNY OGG —and a pile of old coffins mouldering in the cellar?

IGOR Yeth, yeth. Look, I'd love to thtop and chat, but I must get thothe bocktheth up to their room. Do exthcuthe me.

IGOR *picks up the boxes and exits.*

VLAD *enters silently and watches.*

NANNY OGG Well, well, so our king invited vampires, did he?

AGNES NITT What'll we do?

NANNY OGG Do? He invited 'em. They're guests.

AGNES NITT But what'll Granny say?

NANNY OGG Look, they'll be gone tomorrow. We'll just keep an eye on 'em and wave 'em goodbye when they go.

VLAD Ladies? I heard you mention vampires. Perhaps I could be of help?

The **DE MAGPYRS, VERENCE** *and* **MAGRAT** *enter.*

NANNY OGG Why?

VLAD Well, I am one. Charmed to meet you, Mrs Ogg. *(He reaches for* **NANNY OGG**'*s hand)*

NANNY OGG *(pulling her hand away)* Getaway! I don't hold with bloodsuckers!

VLAD I know. But I'm sure you will in time.

NANNY OGG You can bugger off. What was the king thinking of?

AGNES NITT Nanny, there's no need to be so rude; I'm sure Vlad isn't going to bite your neck.

VLAD Of course not. We had some sort of bandit on the way here.

NANNY OGG You what?

AGNES NITT You just killed someone?

VLAD Of course. We are vampires. Though we spell it with a "y", not an "i". It's far more modern. Now, do come and meet Father.

AGNES NITT You actually killed someone?

NANNY OGG Right! That's it! I'm gonna get Shawn and he's gonna come back with a big sharp—

VLAD *waves his hand casually in front of* **NANNY OGG,** *stopping her in her tracks.*

VLAD There are several other things people know about vampires. And one is that they have considerable control over the minds of lesser creatures. So forget all about vampires, dear ladies. That is an order. Now come and meet the family.

NANNY OGG *(slightly stunned)* Seems a nice young man.

AGNES NITT I – er – yes.

PERDITA Wh...

AGNES NITT I wish Granny was here.

NANNY OGG She ain't much good at parties.

AGNES NITT *and* **NANNY OGG** *move across to* **VERENCE** *and the* **COUNT.**

VERENCE Ah, Agnes and Nanny. Count, can I present—

A flash of lightning and a clap of thunder.

COUNT Gytha Ogg and Agnes Nitt, I believe. Allow me to introduce the Countess de Magpyr. These are the witches I told you about, dear. I believe you have met my son? And this is my daughter, Lacrimosa.

VERENCE The count was telling me how he is planning to move into the castle and rule the country. And I was saying we shall be honoured.

NANNY OGG Well done.

COUNT The trouble is that people always think of vampires in terms of their diet. You eat animal flesh and vegetables, but it hardly defines you, does it?

VERENCE But you do drink human blood?

COUNT Of course. And sometimes we kill people. Though hardly at all, these days. But where is the harm in that? Hunter and prey, prey and hunter. Just part of the great cycle of nature.

VERENCE Fascinating.

COUNTESS Of course, in Überwald everyone knows all this instinctively. But it is a rather backward place for the children. We are so looking forward to Lancre. And so very kind of you to invite us. Otherwise, we could not have come, of course.

The band strikes up, off.

VLAD Do you dance, Miss Nitt?

The dance begins. **VLAD** *dances with* **AGNES NITT,** *the* **COUNTESS** *with* **VERENCE,** *the* **COUNT** *with* **MAGRAT.** **LACRIMOSA** *stands and scowls.* **NANNY OGG,** *under the* **VAMPIRE** *influence, just stands and smiles.*

AGNES NITT Ur...not really. Not very well—

PERDITA Didn't you listen to what they said? They're vampires!

AGNES NITT Shut up!

VLAD I beg your pardon?

AGNES NITT —and they're not - er -a very good orchestra—

PERDITA Didn't you pay any attention at all, you useless lump?

VLAD They're a very bad orchestra.

AGNES NITT Well, the king only bought the instruments last month and, er—

PERDITA Chop his head off! Give him a garlic enema!

VLAD Are you all right? You do know there are no vampires here, don't you?

PERDITA He's controlling you! They're affecting people!

AGNES NITT I'm a bit faint from all the excitement. I think I'll go home. I'll ask Nanny to go with me.

VLAD *and* **AGNES NITT** *stop dancing.*

VLAD *(puzzled)* I don't think I've ever met anyone quite like you, Miss Nitt. There's something so—inner about you.

The COUNT *and* COUNTESS *stop dancing and watch* AGNES NITT. *Their partners stand immobile.*

PERDITA That's me! That's me! He can't work me out! Now let's both get out of here!

AGNES NITT *moves to* NANNY OGG, *who snaps out of her reverie.*

AGNES NITT Could you – help us – me home, Nanny?

NANNY OGG Are you all right?

AGNES NITT We – I feel terrible.

NANNY OGG Well, all the beer's gone, so there's not much point in stoppin'. Come on then.

VLAD We shall meet again, Agnes Nitt.

The music stops.

Blackout.

Scene Six
The Road Back To Agnes's Cottage

Night. An owl hoots. The wind soughs in the trees.

NANNY OGG *and* **AGNES NITT** *(and* **PERDITA***) enter.*

AGNES NITT *is arguing with herself,* **PERDITA** *miming her part of the conversation.*

AGNES NITT Yes, yes, all right, I'll tell her! Yes! Yes! All right, just shut up will y... Look, it's my body, you're just a figment of my... OK! OK! Perhaps it isn't that simple, but just let me talk to Nanny, will you?

NANNY OGG What's going on, my girl? Who are you talkin'to?

AGNES NITT Myself. Well, to my courageous side, really – Perdita.

NANNY OGG Oh yes – your flash name. Perdita X. Nitt.

AGNES NITT Well anyway she's been advising me and... And I'm not too fat, thank you very much!

NANNY OGG How many of you are there in there?

AGNES NITT *(to* **PERDITA***)* What do you mean, "Room for ten"? Shut up! *(To* **NANNY***)* Listen, Perdita says there were vampires at the castle party. The Magpyr family, she says. They put some kind of 'fluence over everyone, she says. Including me, which is how she was able to... *(To* **PERDITA***)* Yes, all right. I'm telling it, thank you!

NANNY OGG Why not her, too, then?

AGNES NITT Because she's got a mind of her own! Can you remember anything they said? Do you remember talking to Igor?

NANNY OGG They seemed very nice people... Who's Igor? Anyhow, why should we believe this Perdita, anyway?

AGNES NITT Because she's me! Inside me.

NANNY OGG (*peering into* **AGNES**'s *mouth*) Hello? How're you doin' in there? Treatin' you all right, is she?

AGNES NITT Ha ha. Very funny. Look, they were eating garlic and saying stuff about killing people and drinking blood and everyone was just smiling and nodding. Even you.

NANNY OGG That can't be right, can it? 'Ere, how does this Perdita thing work, then?

AGNES NITT Look, you know the part of you that wants to do all the things you don't dare to, and thinks the thoughts you don't dare think...?

NANNY OGG *looks blank.*

Like – maybe – rip off all your clothes and run naked in the rain? Well, Perdita is that part of me.

NANNY OGG I've always been that part of me. The important thing is to remember where you left your clothes. I think I know what you mean, though. She's the thin girl; you're the chocolate.

AGNES NITT Well... Yes, sort of. I suppose.

NANNY OGG But... Vampires. Right. They won't have left the castle yet. I'll round up Shawn and Jason and the lads, and then we'll—

AGNES NITT Won't work. The moment you get near them, you'll forget all about it. They do something to your mind. Perdita thinks they can tell what you're thinking, too.

NANNY OGG This is Esme's sort of stuff. Messing with minds and so on. It's meat and drink to her. She ought to be sortin' this out.

AGNES NITT Nanny, they were talking about staying! We have to do something! Maybe they've already got to Granny!

NANNY OGG You think so? I can't think about a vampire gettin' his teeth into Esme.

PERDITA
AGNES NITT } *(together)* Don't worry, dog doesn't eat dog.

AGNES NITT *clasps her hand over her mouth.*

NANNY *grabs* **AGNES NITT** *by the scruff of the neck.*

NANNY OGG I ain't normally given to physicality but you keep a civil tongue in your heads, my girl, or we'll fall out. OK? Now, we're goin' back to the castle to sort this out right now! I've learned a thing or two from Esme.

AGNES NITT Yes, but she's bet...she's not here.

NANNY OGG That's as maybe. But I'd rather face them now than try to explain to Esme why I didn't. Come on.

Blackout.

Scene Seven
Lancre Castle

SHAWN OGG *enters.*

SHAWN OGG His Majesty, Verence II, King of Lancre.

VERENCE *enters, with the* **COUNT, COUNTESS, VLAD** *and* **LACRIMOSA.**

VERENCE Yes, all right, thank you, Shawn.

SHAWN OGG *exits.*

You were saying, count?

COUNT Yes, I was saying that, even though Lancre will become a duchy of my lands in Überwald, it will still be referred to as a kingdom.

VERENCE That is very reasonable of you, I must say.

COUNT There will be taxes, of course. Not onerous. We don't want blood – figuratively speaking.

The **VAMPIRES** *laugh.* **VERENCE,** *largely under their spell, smiles in a rather strained way.*

SHAWN OGG *enters.*

SHAWN OGG The Mistresses Gytha Ogg and—

NANNY OGG *enters with* **AGNES NITT** *in tow, barging past* **SHAWN OGG.**

SHAWN OGG *exits.*

NANNY OGG Aha! Count de Magpyr, I believe?

COUNT Ladies, I was just congratulating King Verence on his modern attitude. People have quite the wrong idea about vampires, you see. Are we fiendish killers? *(He smiles)* Well, yes, of course we are. But only when necessary. We could hardly hope to rule a country if we went round killing people all the time, now could we? For one thing, there'd be no one left to rule!

There is polite laughter.

VLAD *crosses to* **AGNES NITT.**

AGNES NITT Coming under the influence. *(To* **NANNY***)* That makes sense, doesn't it? Very fair minded. Anyone who doesn't think so deserves to die, in my view.

PERDITA They've got you again.

COUNTESS We are only human. Well – in fact, not only human. But if you prick us, do we not bleed? Which always seems such a waste.

COUNT We are, above all, up to date. And we do like what you've done to this castle, I must say.

COUNTESS Oh, those guttering torches back home and some of the things in the dungeons so fifteenth century. I nearly died of shame. We're not ashamed of what we are. We all have needs, after all.

PERDITA You're standing around like rabbits in front of a fox!

VERENCE *(in a strained voice)* Yes, yes, of course.

PERDITA He's trying to fight it! Now aren't you glad you've got me?

VLAD You are a fascinating woman, Miss Nitt. Such lovely hair. But, who is Perdita?

AGNES NITT No one really.

PERDITA He can see what you're thinking.

VLAD You can resist, can't you? Do you have any vampire blood in you?

AGNES NITT Certainly not!

VLAD It could be arranged. *(He laughs)* Look at Mrs Ogg. Grinning like a pumpkin. And she is apparently one of the more powerful witches hereabouts. Pathetic.

PERDITA Tell him you know he can read minds!

AGNES NITT You can—

VLAD No, not exactly. Just people. Things will be changing, Miss Nitt. Father is right. We're vampires. Why be ashamed of it? We were born vampires.

AGNES NITT I thought you lot became—

VLAD —vampires by being bitten? Dear me, no. Oh, we can turn people into vampires that way, but what's the point? I mean, when you eat – oh yes, chocolate – you don't want it turning into another Agnes Nitt, do you? *(He sighs)* We have great hopes of Lancre. After some re-decoration.

AGNES NITT You're taking our country – just like that?

VLAD Oh yes. A bloodless coup. Metaphorically. You really are quite remarkable, Miss Nitt. The Überwald girls are so sheeplike. But you...you're concealing something from me. I think you're under my power but something tells me you're not. This is delightful...

> PERDITA *forces* AGNES NITT*'s hand up to strike* VLAD.

PERDITA Oh for God's sake...

> VLAD *catches* AGNES NITT*'s hand before it makes contact. She tries again with the other, which he also catches.*

VLAD Well done. I like a woman with spirit!

> AGNES NITT *brings her knee up and embeds it in* VLAD*'s groin.*

(doubling up) Ghni... *(Crumpling; hoarsely)* Magnificent...

AGNES NITT *(moving to NANNY)* Nanny, we're leaving!

NANNY OGG *(dreamily)* Are we, dear?

AGNES NITT Nanny?

PERDITA For goodness' sake, Agnes, I wish I read as many books as you. What do you use against vampires?

COUNTESS *(catching the edge of* AGNES'*s thought)* Daylight is good, my dear. *(To the* COUNT*)* Our uncle always had big windows and easily-twitched curtains, didn't he, dear?

COUNT Yes, indeed.

COUNTESS And when it came to running water, he always kept the moat flowing perfectly, didn't he?

COUNT Fed from a mountain stream, I believe.

COUNTESS And the castle was simply stuffed with ornaments that could be bent or broken into some kind of religious symbol or other?

COUNT Yes. He was a vampire of the old school.

COUNTESS Yes, the stupid school. *(To* AGNES *and* PERDITA*)* So I think you will find we are here to stay, my dear. Although you do seem to have made an impression on my son. Come here, girl, and let me have a look at you.

The COUNTESS *gestures and* AGNES NITT *and* PERDITA *move across to her as if propelled by an invisible force.*

AGNES NITT Where's Magrat?

COUNTESS Putting the baby to bed, I believe. A lovely child.

AGNES NITT Granny Weatherwax is going to hear about this.

The COUNT *gestures and* AGNES NITT *is moved across to him.*

COUNT Oh I do hope so. We are looking forward to meeting her. *(Smooth as silk)* Perhaps you should go and fetch her? Take your friend. And when you see her, Miss Nitt, you can tell her that there is no reason why witches and vampires should fight. Go. To her cottage. Get her.

The COUNT *gestures.* NANNY OGG, AGNES NITT *and* PERDITA *are propelled to the door. At the last moment,* PERDITA *turns* AGNES NITT *to face the* COUNT *again.*

AGNES NITT *(with an effort)* We'll – be – back!

NANNY OGG, AGNES NITT *and* **PERDITA** *exit.*

COUNT Good. We are famous for our hospitality.

The **VAMPIRES** *laugh.*

Blackout.

Scene Eight
Granny's Cottage

Inside the cottage. It seems empty. The table is laid with three sets of knives, forks, spoons and cups.

AGNES NITT *(offstage)* Granny?

    AGNES NITT *enters.*

Granny? Are you here?

    NANNY OGG *enters from within the cottage.*

NANNY OGG She's gorn.

AGNES NITT Gone? Just when we need her? Perhaps she's just out?

NANNY OGG Bin gone at least two hours, if I'm any judge.

AGNES NITT But how...?

NANNY OGG First thing she does each day, rain or shine, wash her face in the water butt. Someone broke the ice on it two hours ago. You can see where it froze over again. And she's left the whole cottage neat. Same all over. Her I ATE'NT DEAD card's hanging behind the door and the guzunda's so clean you could drink your tea out of it. Stuff all laid out on the table and dresser. And she's taken the box.

AGNES NITT What box?

NANNY OGG You know. Where she keeps her memorabilia. Keepsakes and whatnot. Stuff that's hers.

AGNES NITT Granny wouldn't go would she? She's always here.

    AGNES NITT *exits further into the cottage.*

NANNY OGG Trouble is. She's been herself recently.

AGNES NITT *(offstage)* You mean she's not been herself.

NANNY OGG I mean what I mean, girl. When she's herself she snaps at people and sulks and makes herself depressed. *(Pause)* Clock's stopped, too. Not that it ever kept good time. She only kept it for the tick.

AGNES NITT *(offstage)* Oh, hello, Mr Magpie. What're you doing in here?

NANNY OGG *moves to the exit* **AGNES** *just used, takes a boiled sweet from her pocket and throws it offstage. We hear the clatter of a magpie's cry.*

NANNY OGG Bugger off, you bastard!

AGNES NITT *(offstage)* That's bad luck.

NANNY OGG Will be for him if 'e comes in range again. Can't bear them maggotty-pies.

AGNES NITT *enters.*

AGNES NITT "One for sorrow, Two for joy, Three for a girl..."

NANNY OGG It's "Two for mirth" in the old version. And three for a funeral"...

AGNES NITT Wait. Look – on the table. Three knives, three forks, three spoons. Three cups.

NANNY OGG Esme's got four cups. Know that for a fact.

AGNES NITT There's a broken one here in the hearth. *(A realisation)* Nanny? Would I be right in thinking that the clock has stopped at three o'clock?

NANNY OGG Just after.

AGNES NITT Three minutes after.

NANNY OGG Well – yes.

AGNES NITT Threes, Nanny. She was thinking in threes. I noticed some other cutlery and stuff in the goatshed as I came in, but she only put out threes.

NANNY OGG "Four for a birth". Bugger. I was hopin' she wouldn't notice. I'll tan my Shawn's hide when I gets back. He swore to me he'd delivered that invite. But it ain't here.

AGNES NITT Maybe she took it with her.

NANNY OGG No. If she'd had it, she would've come last night. No, the threes is because of the baby.

AGNES NITT What do you mean?

NANNY OGG Magrat's got a daughter. She's a mother! I can't start being a hag at my time of life! None of my bras'll fit!

AGNES NITT Nanny, what are you talking about?

NANNY OGG It's this business of three witches, you know. The maiden, the mother and the crone. You see, you're a maiden, ain't you?

AGNES NITT Nanny!

NANNY OGG Well, I knows you is,' cos I'd have heard by now if'n you wasn't. And Magrat's a mother... I reckon she's thinks there's a new three here. That bloody invitation must've been the last straw. So she's gone. Can't say I fancy bein' a crone. I ain't the right shape and I ain't sure what sound they make.

AGNES NITT But Granny isn't a... Wasn't a... I mean, she didn't look like a...

NANNY OGG *(simply)* There's no point in lookin' at a dog and sayin' that's not a dog 'cos a dog don't look like that.

AGNES NITT She thinks we don't need her any more?

NANNY OGG I reckon so.

AGNES NITT What about the vampires? The two of us can't cope with them!

NANNY OGG Three.

AGNES NITT Magrat? But she's no Nanny Ogg!

NANNY OGG Well, I sure as hell ain't Granny Weather wax, come to that. Gettin' inside people's heads. Puttin' her mind someplace else. That's her fortay.

AGNES NITT Maybe we weren't always nice to her.

NANNY OGG Esme didn't thrive on nice. Take her an apple pie, she'd complain about the pastry. To tell the truth, there's always been a bit of dark about the Weatherwaxes. That's where the trouble is. Look at old Alison Weatherwax, Esme's gran. Went to the bad, they say. Just packed up and headed for Überwald one day. That's why Esme's always standin' behind herself and criticisin' what's she's doin. Terrified of goin' bad.

AGNES NITT But Granny's as moral a person as I know.

NANNY OGG Yes. That's because she's got Granny Weatherwax lookin' over her shoulder all the time.

AGNES NITT Did she know Magrat was going to call the baby Esme?

NANNY OGG Prob'ly. Doesn't miss much.

AGNES NITT Not too tactful, in some ways. Perhaps she thought the name was being passed on. Inherited.

NANNY OGG Yes. That could send her off into one. (*She sees something in the cottage*)

We hear the magpies again.

That bloody magpie's back. And it's got one of her napkin rings! Oy! Bugger off!

NANNY OGG *moves downstage, "out" of the cottage.*

Too late! It's taken it up into the crab apple tree!

AGNES NITT (*following* **NANNY OGG**) I'll get it. That's an easy climb.

PERDITA In your dreams!

AGNES NITT *comes "out" of the cottage and exits upstage.*

We hear the rustling of the tree as AGNES NITT *climbs it.*

NANNY *watches.*

NANNY OGG   Can you see it yet?

AGNES NITT   *(puffing; offstage)* Give me a moment, will you?

There is the sound of cloth ripping.

Oh no!

NANNY OGG   What?

AGNES NITT   *(offstage)* I think my drawers have split.

NANNY OGG   Good thing, roomy drawers.

PERDITA   Lump. I could've climbed this like a gazelle!

AGNES NITT   *(offstage)* Gazelles don't climb trees!

NANNY OGG   What?

AGNES NITT   *(offstage)* Nothing.

AGNES *appears on the balcony, as if up the tree.*

Ah. Here we are. This looks like quite an old nest. *(To herself easing towards the nest)* ...Five for silver, six for gold...

NANNY OGG   Five for heaven, Six for hell!

AGNES NITT   Got it!

There is the sound of wood breaking.

AGNES NITT *disappears.*

(offstage) Aah!

A thump. A pause.

AGNES NITT *stumbles on, carrying* GRANNY's *invitation, a heavily gold-trimmed card.* NANNY *takes the invitation and examines it.*

NANNY OGG Too much gold. Them birds'll nick anything that glitters.

AGNES NITT I'm not hurt at all, thank you for asking. The holly bush cushioned my fall.

There are more magpie cries.

NANNY OGG *(looking up, as if at circling birds)* I'll wring their ruddy necks.

AGNES NITT I might have dislocated my hat, though. *(She sighs)* Oh well. So – we've found the invitation. It was all a terrible misunderstanding. Now let's find Granny.

NANNY OGG Not if she don't want to be found.

AGNES NITT You can do Borrowing. There must be some forest creatures that saw her...

NANNY OGG Dodgy, that. I was a rabbit for three days, once. Our Jason had to fetch Esme to get me back.

AGNES NITT Rabbits sound dull.

OATS *enters.*

NANNY OGG They have their ups and downs... Oh hell, what's he doin' here?

OATS Ah, Mrs Ogg... Miss Nitt. I had hoped to find Mrs Weatherwax.

AGNES NITT Hoped?

NANNY OGG *Mrs* Weatherwax?

OATS Er, yes. It's part of my... One of those things I... We... Well, I heard she might be ill, and visiting the elderly and infirm is a part of our pastoral duties...

NANNY OGG I'm really sorry she ain't here. I'm sure she'd be all the better for a visit from you. It'd be the sort of thing she'd talk about for days.

OATS Well, I suppose I'd better be getting back to town, then. Can I accompany you ladies? There are some dangerous things in the woods.

NANNY OGG I got me broomstick.

AGNES NITT I'll walk back with you.

NANNY OGG See you back at my place. No dilly-dallying.

AGNES NITT I don't dilly-dally.

NANNY OGG Just see to it you don't start.

NANNY OGG *exits.*

AGNES NITT How's the head cold?

OATS Oh, much better, thank you. Her majesty gave me some pills.

PERDITA She ought to have given him a needle! Look at the size of that boil! Why doesn't he do something about it?

OATS You don't like me much, do you?

AGNES NITT I've hardly met you.

OATS A lot of people don't like me as soon as they've met me.

PERDITA That must save time. Don't get involved with this twerp.

OATS Everything seemed much clearer at college. All the parables and so on. But here everyone is so literal. They say things like, "That's stupid way to run a vineyard" or "Mushrooms don't grow in the desert." *(He clears his throat)* Unfortunately, the Book of Om is somewhat unyielding on the subject of witches.

AGNES NITT Really?

OATS Although, after much research, I have advanced the rather daring theory that the actual word in question translates more accurately as "cockroaches".

AGNES NITT Yes?

OATS Especially since it goes on to say that they can be killed in traps of treacle. It goes on to say that they bring lascivious dreams.

AGNES NITT Don't look at me. All you're getting is a walk home!

OATS Er...the word in question could also be translated as "boiled lobsters".

AGNES NITT Why did you come to visit Granny Weatherwax?

OATS Well, everyone speaks very highly of her. And they say she didn't turn up last night. And I thought it must be hard for an old lady living on her own. And...

AGNES NITT So – someone told you about Granny Weatherwax and you still walked through these scary woods to see her, even though she might turn out to be a cockroach or a boiled lobster!

OATS A cockroach is nothing compared with the vampires you have here.

AGNES NITT Vampires? You saw the vampires?

OATS Yes of course. We studied them at the seminary, but I never expected to actually see them walking about, drinking blood; really I' m surprised the king allows it...

AGNES NITT And they didn't affect your mind?

OATS I did have a terrible migraine. Does that count?

A wolf howls, off.

What the heck was that?

AGNES NITT I don't know, but I don't think we really want to find out. Come on, let's get back.

Both exit hurriedly.

Blackout.

Scene Nine
Lancre Castle

It is dawn.

A window-frame gobo casts the light from a window in the fourth wall on to the stage downstage centre. A bell rope hangs down by the wall.

The DE MAGPYR *family walk on and into the light.* LACRIMOSA *is carrying four wine glasses.* VLAD *is carrying a bottle of red wine and fiddles with the corkscrew during the opening dialogue.*

COUNT There, you see? Morning, and we're still here.

LACRIMOSA You've made it overcast. It's hardly sunny.

COUNT One step at a time, my dear. Today, yes, it is overcast, but we can build on it. We can acclimatise. And one day – the beach.

COUNTESS You really are very clever, my dear.

COUNT Thank you, my love. How are you doing with that, Vlad?

VLAD Is this such a good idea, Father? I thought we did not drink – wine.

COUNT I believe it's time we started.

VLAD *pours the wine.*

LACRIMOSA Yuk! I'm not touching that! It's squeezed from vegetables!

COUNT Fruit, I think you'll find. You'll try some, my dear?

COUNTESS Do we, er... Are we, um, supposed to warm it first?

COUNT Room temperature is suggested.

LACRIMOSA That's sickening!

COUNTESS Try it for your father, dear. Quickly, before it congeals.

COUNT No, my dear. Wine stays runny.

COUNTESS Really? How very convenient. *(To* **VLAD,** *who is looking askance at his glass)* Perhaps it would help if you think of it as grape's blood. *(To* **LACRIMOSA***)* Lacci? I thought you'd like this sort of thing, dear. It's the sort of thing your "crowd" does, isn't it?

LACRIMOSA I don't know what you're talking about!

COUNTESS Oh, staying up til gone noon, wearing bright clothes – and giving yourselves funny names...

VLAD Like Brenda. And Susan. They think it's cool.

LACRIMOSA That's none of your business!

COUNTESS Lady Strigouil said her daughter has taken to calling herself Wendy. I mean, Heiroglyphica is such a nice name. And if I was her mother I'd see to it she wore at least a bit of eyeliner...

LACRIMOSA Yes, but no one drinks wine. Only real weirdos who file their teeth flat drink wine.

VLAD Maladora Kroyjek does. Or Daisy I should say...

LACRIMOSA She does not!

VLAD What? She wears a silver corkscrew on a chain round her neck!

LACRIMOSA That's just a fashion item! I know she says she's partial to a drop of port, but really it's blood in the glass. Henry actually brought wine to a party once and she fainted at the smell.

COUNTESS Henry?

LACRIMOSA *(sulkily)* Graven Guirachi.

VLAD The one who grows his hair short and pretends he's a chartered accountant.

COUNT Be quiet. This is all just cultural conditioning. I've worked hard for this. All we want is a piece of the day. Is that too much to ask? And wine is just wine. Now, take up your glasses. You, too, Lacci. Please? For Daddy?

VLAD And when you tell "Cyril" and "Tim" they'll be so impressed!

COUNT Please?

LACRIMOSA Oh, well...

COUNT Good.

> *They drink. They all shudder.*

There. That wasn't too bad, now, was it?

VLAD A bit chilly.

COUNT I'll have a wine warmer installed. I am not an unreasonable vampire. *(Suddenly he produces from his pocket a card with a religious symbol on it)*

> *None of the family reacts.*

Well done!

VLAD *(with a bored expression)* It's the Double Snake Symbol of the Tsortean Water Cult.

COUNT You see? You barely flinched! Sacrephobia can be beaten!

LACRIMOSA I hated the way you used to leap out of the shadows and flick holy water over us.

COUNT It was strongly diluted. But it made you strong, didn't it?

LACRIMOSA I caught lots of colds. I remember that.

> *The* **COUNT** *whips out another card.*

The All-Seeing Face of the Ionians.

COUNT You see! You didn't even wince! And as religious symbols go, it's pretty strong. Isn't it all worth it?

LACRIMOSA There'll have to be something really good to make up for those garlic pillows you made us sleep on.

COUNT (*moving to* LACRIMOSA) Will it be enough to know that the world is your oyster?

LACRIMOSA We-ell...

COUNT Good. Now, who shall we have for breakfast?

LACRIMOSA The baby.

COUNT No, I think not. That would be undiplomatic. We're not quite there yet.

LACRIMOSA Well, that apology for a queen looks pretty bloodless. Vlad should have hung on to his plump girl...

VLAD Don't start. Agnes is a very – interesting girl. I feel there is a lot in her...

LACRIMOSA A lot *of* her, you mean.

COUNT Now, now, children. Your own dear mother wasn't a vampire when we first met.

LACRIMOSA Yes, yes, you've told us a million times...

VLAD The balcony, the nightdress, you in your cloak...

COUNT (*with a sigh*) Things were simpler then. Where the hell's Igor?

COUNTESS Ah, I've been meaning to talk to you about him, my dear. I think he'll have to go.

LACRIMOSA That's right! Even my friends laugh at him!

COUNTESS I find his more-Gothic-than-thou attitude extremely irritating. That stupid accent. And do you know what I caught him doing in the dungeons last week?

COUNT I'm sure I couldn't guess.

COUNTESS He had a box of spiders and a whip! He was training them to spin webs all over the place!

COUNT I did wonder why there were always so many.

VLAD He's all right for Überwald, but you'd hardly want him opening the door in polite society, would you?

COUNTESS And he smells.

COUNT Of course, parts of him have been in the family for centuries. But I must admit he is getting beyond a joke. *(He pulls the bell rope)*

IGOR *appears immediately, startling the* COUNT.

IGOR Yeth, marthter?

COUNT I told you to stop doing that!

IGOR What, marthter?

COUNT Turning up behind me like that!

IGOR It'th the only way I know how to turn up, marthter.

COUNT Go and fetch King Verence, will you?

IGOR Yeth, marthter.

IGOR *limps off.*

VLAD He'll never retire. He'll never take the hint.

COUNTESS It's so old-fashioned, having a servant called Igor.

LACRIMOSA Look, it's simple. Take him down to the dungeon, slam him in the Iron Maiden, stretch him on the rack over a fire for a few days, and then slice him thinly from the feet upwards, so he can watch. You'll be doing him a kindness, really.

COUNT I suppose it's the best way.

LACRIMOSA I remember when you told me to put my cat out of its misery.

COUNT I really meant for you to stop what you were doing to it. But yes, you are right, he'll have to go.

IGOR *and* **VERENCE** *enter.*

IGOR Hith Royal Highneth King Verenthe of Lancre.

COUNTESS Ah, your majesty. Do join us in a light meal.

Blackout.

Scene Ten
The Road To Lancre Castle

A stone-faced peasant, under the **VAMPIRES**' *spell, enters and heads across the stage.*

NANNY OGG *bustles on.*

NANNY OGG *(to the peasant; breezily)* Wotcha!

The peasant ignores her and exits.

(looking after the peasant; muttering) Sod yer then.

AGNES NITT, PERDITA *and* **OATS** *enter, breathlessly.*

NANNY OGG You two were a long time. Bin dallyin'?

AGNES NITT Nanny, Granny would have said that.

NANNY OGG *(with a shudder)* You're right, girl. Let's find her quickly, eh? I'm too cheerful to be a crone.

AGNES NITT Granny was seen up above the long lake.

NANNY OGG On that bit of moor?

AGNES NITT Yes.

NANNY OGG That's bad. That's gnarly country up there.

AGNES NITT Gnarly?

NANNY OGG All scrunched up. Strong magical force, you see. She'll have gone up there to stop the vampires from tracking her down.

AGNES NITT What? I've been up there. It's just heather and gorse and there's some old caves at the end of the valley.

NANNY OGG Oh really? Well, you'll soon see. This is going to need the three of us. Especially if she is up there. Gnarly ground plays merry hell with scrying. We just ain't got the power.

AGNES NITT I don't want to go back to the castle!

NANNY OGG Magrat's good at that sort of thing.

AGNES NITT She's got a little baby to look after, Nanny.

NANNY OGG In a castle full of vampires. Think about that. No knowing when they'll get hungry again.

AGNES NITT But—

NANNY OGG You get her out now. I'd come meself, but you said I just stand there grinnin'.

AGNES NITT *(pointing at* **OATS***)* You!

OATS Me?

AGNES NITT You said you could see they were vampires, didn't you?

OATS I did?

AGNES NITT You did!

OATS Er – and...?

AGNES NITT You didn't find your mind going all pink and happy?

OATS I don't think my mind's ever been pink and happy.

AGNES NITT So why didn't they get to you?

OATS I am protected by the hand of Om. He will spread his wings over me in times of trial.

AGNES NITT That's handy. Well, you're coming with me to the castle, Mr Oats. I'm not facing Prince Slime again alone! *(To* **PERDITA***)* And you can shut up!

OATS Me? Why...?

AGNES NITT No, not you. Never mind. Look, you said you'd studied vampires. What's good for vampires, then?

OATS Well, nice dry coffin, er, plenty of fresh blood, um, overcast skies, er...

AGNES *looks irritated.*

(seeing **AGNES***'s expression)* Oh. Ah. Right. Well, it depends where they're from. Überwald is a very big place. Cutting their head off and/or staking them through the heart is generally thought to be efficacious.

NANNY OGG But that would work on anyone.

OATS Er – in Splintz they die if you cut their head off and put a coin in their mouth.

NANNY OGG Oh, not like ordinary people then.

OATS Er – in Klotz they die if you put a lemon in their mouth—

NANNY OGG Ah, that sounds more like it!

OATS —after you've cut their head off. In Glitz you have to fill their mouth with salt, hammer a carrot into both ears and then cut off their head.

NANNY OGG I can see that must have been fun finding out.

OATS And in the valley of the river ah, you're supposed to boil the severed head in vinegar. And then, of course, you can defeat them by stealing their left sock.

AGNES NITT Pardon me?

OATS They're pathologically meticulous, you see. Some of the gypsy tribes say they'll spend the rest of eternity looking for it. In some villages they say that you can slow them down by throwing poppy seeds at them. They'll have a terrible urge to count every seed. Vampires are very anally retentive, you see.

NANNY OGG I don't think I'd like to meet one that wasn't! Why are you such an expert, anyway?

OATS I studied it at college. You have to know the enemy if you're going to fight evil forces – vampires, demons, wit...

NANNY OGG *(very sweetly)* Do go on.

OATS Um.

NANNY OGG Off you go, then. All three of you.

OATS Three of us? What does she mean?

AGNES NITT, PERDITA *and* **OATS** *head for the exit.*

AGNES NITT *(loudly, as they exit)* Ignore her. Her mind's wandering!

Blackout.

Scene Eleven
A Balcony In The Castle Tower

There are the sounds of flapping wings and the cries of magpies in flight.

The COUNT *is on the balcony, looking over the railings. We hear the* COUNT*'s thoughts over the speakers.*

COUNT DE MAGPYR *(voiceover)* This is the way to run a country. You need to get so close to humans to be able to read their minds clearly. Much better to send out the magpies as spies. The birds can go anywhere. Almost anywhere. They see every worker in the fields, every hunter in the forest. Much better listeners than bats or rats. Another break with the old traditions. No sign of Granny Weatherwax, though. Some trick perhaps. It doesn't matter. Sooner or later, she'll find me. She won't hide for long. Not in her nature. Weatherwaxes will always stand and fight, even when they know they'll be beaten. So predictable.

COUNT So very predictable.

Blackout.

Scene Twelve
A Room In Lancre Castle

AGNES NITT, PERDITA *and* OATS *enter.*

A couple of castle servants, mufflers wrapped around their necks, cross the stage, stone-faced, and pass AGNES NITT, PERDITA *and* OATS *without acknowledging their presence.*

AGNES NITT Either there's a plague of sore throats or there'll be some nasty little puncture wounds under those scarves, I'll be bound.

OATS Er, I do know a bit about the way they control people. It sounds a bit silly. It was an old book...

AGNES NITT What?

OATS They find single-minded people easier to control. It doesn't sound right, I know. You'd think strong-minded people would be harder to affect. I suppose a big target is easier to hit. In some villages, vampire hunters get roaring drunk first. Muddles their mind up. Protection, you see? You can't punch fog.

OATS *freezes during* AGNES NITT*'s and* PERDITA*'s next little exchange.*

PERDITA So we're fog, are we? So's he, by the look of him. Thick and wet.

AGNES NITT They're like cattle. One man can easily control a herd of cows, even though any one of them is quite capable of crushing him flat. It's just they never get round to thinking about it. So I suppose the vampires are better than us, really. Compared to them, we're just—

PERDITA You're too close to them. You're thinking cow thoughts!

AGNES NITT *(to* OATS*)* Come on, then. Nanny Ogg says you must seize time by the foreskin!

OATS She does?

AGNES NITT I'm afraid so. You get used to it. Come on, let's get on with it. *(She moves to the exit)* Hide! Their servant's coming!

AGNES NITT, PERDITA *and* **OATS** *conceal themselves behind the onstage curtain.*

IGOR *enters.*

IGOR *(muttering)* Ged rid of me, would they? Thith will end in tearth. When they get thtaked, who'th going to thweep up the dutht, eh? Who'th going to find them under the ithe? I mutht have pulled out more thtakes than I've had wriggly dinnerth.

The curtain twitches. **IGOR** *sees this and chuckles. He pulls back the curtain to reveal* **AGNES NITT** *and* **PERDITA.**

Oh, look. A vampire hunter, methinkth. Got garlic, have you?

OATS *enters from behind the onstage curtain, brandishing an iron poker. He creeps up behind* **IGOR.**

AGNES NITT Masses.

IGOR Won't work. Any holy water?

AGNES NITT Gallons.

IGOR It—

OATS *strikes* **IGOR** *on the head. He crumples to the ground.*

Oh thit!

OATS I did it! I smote him mightily!

AGNES NITT So you did. Now let's hide him before he's seen. Come on.

AGNES NITT *and* **OATS** *bundle* **IGOR** *offstage.*

(offstage) Quick!

AGNES NITT *enters.*

MRS SCORBIC, *the cook, enters behind* **AGNES NITT.** *She seems unaware of what's going on.*

MRS SCORBIC Agnes?

AGNES NITT *(startled)* Oh! Mrs Scorbic? Hello. How are you feeling?

MRS SCORBIC All the better for you asking, miss.

AGNES NITT All these visitors keeping you busy, are they?

MRS SCORBIC Oh, yes, miss.

AGNES NITT And, er, what did you give them for breakfast?

MRS SCORBIC *(frowning)* Can't remember, miss.

AGNES NITT Oh well, never mind. Well, don't let me keep you from – whatever it was you were doing.

MRS SCORBIC Thank you, miss.

MRS SCORBIC *exits.*

PERDITA Plenty of meals in her. Cook and larder all in one.

AGNES NITT That's tasteless!

OATS *enters.*

OATS What was?

AGNES NITT Sorry. Just thinking out loud. Come on.

AGNES NITT, PERDITA *and* **OATS** *head for the exit.*

MAGRAT GARLICK *enters, with the baby.*

MAGRAT GARLICK Agnes? What are you doing here?

AGNES NITT *(rushing to* **MAGRAT GARLICK***)* Magrat! We need you to come with us! Right now!

MAGRAT GARLICK Why?

AGNES NITT Why? Why? Magrat, there's vampires in the castle! The de Magpyr family are vampires!

MAGRAT GARLICK Don't be silly, they're very pleasant people. I was talking to the countess this very morning...

AGNES NITT What about? I bet you can't remember!

MAGRAT GARLICK I am queen, Agnes!

AGNES NITT Sorry, your majesty, but they affect people's minds.

MAGRAT GARLICK Yours?

AGNES NITT Er, no, it seems I'm, um, immune.

MAGRAT GARLICK *(sharply)* And his?

OATS I am protected by my faith in Om.

MAGRAT GARLICK Is he?

AGNES NITT Apparently.

MAGRAT GARLICK This is silly, Agnes. I'm a married woman, I'm queen, I've got a little baby. I have guests to attend to...

AGNES NITT Your guests are vampires! Your majesty.

MAGRAT GARLICK Yes, but—

AGNES NITT We think Granny Weatherwax is in very bad trouble. Nanny Ogg is very worried. She says it needs the three of us to find Granny.

MAGRAT GARLICK Yes, but—

AGNES NITT And Granny's taken the box, whatever that means.

MAGRAT GARLICK The one from the dresser? Right. *(To* OATS*)* You go through there to the nursery – second on the right – and find a bag. Empty in all the stuff from the top drawer. And take the potty and the little truck, oh, and the stuffed animals and the bag of nappies, and the bag for used nappies, and the bath, and the bag with the towels, and the musical box – oh, and the woolly hat—

AGNES NITT Do we need all of that?

MAGRAT GARLICK Oh yes. Goon!

> **OATS** *exits.*

AGNES NITT Even the toys?

MAGRAT GARLICK Stimulus at an early age is vital to a growing brain. *(She goes to the door and calls after* **OATS***)* And the rubber duck. Oh, and the sponge shaped like a teddy bear. And the teddy bear in the shape of a sponge.

AGNES NITT Why is Granny's box so important?

MAGRAT GARLICK What? Oh – it's just important to her.

AGNES NITT It's magical?

MAGRAT GARLICK No. I don't think so. But everything in it belongs to her, you see. Not to the cottage.

> **OATS** *enters, carrying some large boxes and bags. He has a fluffy bunny clenched in his teeth.*

Have we forgotten anything?

OATS *(spitting out the bunny)* Possibly the ceiling.

MAGRAT GARLICK Then let's go.

> *They all exit.*

> *Blackout.*

Scene Thirteen
A Balcony In Lancre Castle

The COUNT *is on the balcony as before.*

The COUNTESS *enters.*

COUNT I think she has gone to ground.

COUNTESS That was remarkably quick. I thought you said she was quite powerful?

COUNT Oh, indeed. But human. And she's getting older. With age comes doubt. All alone in that barren cottage, no company but the candlelight. It's so simple to open the cracks and let the mind turn in on itself. Like when the wind changes in a forest fire and suddenly it's roaring down on all the houses you thought you'd built so strongly.

COUNTESS So graphically put.

COUNT Thank you.

COUNTESS You were so successful in Escrow.

COUNT A model for the future. Vampires and humans in harmony at last. There is no need for this animosity, as I have always said. Every day, in every way, we get better and better. Positive thinking. Training. Familiarity. Garlic? A pleasant seasoning. Lemons? An acquired taste. Why yesterday, I mislaid a sock and I don't care. I have lots of socks... The word "but" is on the tip of your tongue.

COUNTESS I was just going to say that there were no witches in Escrow.

COUNT The place is better for it! Verence was strangely right, my dear. There's a new world coming and there's no room in it for witches. They are unfitted for survival! Witches? I'm afraid witches are all in the past now.

Blackout.

Scene Fourteen
The Gnarly Ground

There is the sound of the wind; mist swirls around.

A bridge made of a stone slab has been set.

NANNY OGG, AGNES NITT, PERDITA *and* **MAGRAT GARLICK** – *with the baby* – *enter.*

MAGRAT GARLICK Are you saying we've got to cross the gnarly ground?

NANNY OGG 'Sright.

AGNES NITT Look. What is gnarly ground?

NANNY OGG There's a lot of magic in these mountains, right? And everyone knows mountains get made when lumps of land bang together, right? Well, when the magic gets trapped you, sort of, get a bit of land where the space is sort of scrunched up, see? It'd be quite big if it could. Like an old hanky that's all folded up small but still big in a different way.

AGNES NITT But I've been here before and it's just moorland!

NANNY OGG You've got to know the right direction. Damn hard to see. It goes all wobbly. Like tryin' to look at somethin' close up and far off at the same time.

MAGRAT GARLICK *(producing a glass ball from the folds of her dress)* Right. Come on, then.

PERDITA I don't like Magrat like this. She's taking charge. She's not cringing like she used to. She's not wet!

AGNES NITT That's because she's a mother. Mothers are only slightly damp.

MAGRAT GARLICK *and* **NANNY OGG** *peer into the ball. They break off, drained of power.*

MAGRAT GARLICK She was lying down. It was all fuzzy.

NANNY OGG She's in one of the caves. And she's trying to keep our thoughts out. Do you see her card?

MAGRAT GARLICK The "I Ate'nt Dead" card? No, I didn't.

NANNY OGG No, of course she left it at the cottage.

MAGRAT GARLICK Just when we need her, she runs away to a cave?

AGNES NITT Does she know we need her? Does she know about the vampires?

MAGRAT GARLICK We'll have to go and ask her.

AGNES NITT But what about the baby?

MAGRAT GARLICK She's quite comfortable. And I think it's quite possible to combine motherhood and a career.

AGNES NITT I thought you'd given up witchcraft?

MAGRAT GARLICK Yes, well. Let's make sure Granny's OK first.

AGNES NITT But I still can't see anything gnarly!

NANNY OGG You've got to get your eye in, but you'll see if it you watch.

MAGRAT GARLICK *(squinting)* Oh – I think I can.

PERDITA I bet she doesn't. I can't.

AGNES NITT Got it! Yes, I see now!

NANNY OGG This way. Hold hands. And shut your eyes.

MAGRAT GARLICK There's no path!

A strobe light comes on; the wind sounds get louder and more smoke billows across the stage. The **THREE WITCHES** *walk on the spot, as if against a strong wind, holding hands and with their eyes shut.*

Where are we now?

NANNY OGG Still here. Attitude's important. Little Esme all wrapped up is she, Magrat?

MAGRAT GARLICK She's asleep.

NANNY OGG Yeh. Just as well, really.

PERDITA Agnes?

AGNES NITT What?

PERDITA Nanny's worried about something to do with the baby and Granny. I think it's to do with her Borrowing.

AGNES NITT What? Granny's using the baby to keep an eye on us?

PERDITA Maybe.

AGNES NITT *(to* **NANNY OGG***)* Nanny? Shouldn't we have found that little stream by now?

There is the sound of a large rushing river.

MAGRAT GARLICK That can't be right! It's wider and deeper than the Lancre gorge!

PERDITA It's a couple of feet deep! I can see every pebble!

AGNES NITT *(to* **NANNY** *and* **MAGRAT***)* Perdita thinks it's an optical illusion!

NANNY OGG She could be right. Gnarly ground, see? Bigger on the inside. We can cross it on the bridge, though. *(She points to the slab)*

MAGRAT GARLICK That's too weak to take our weight!

PERDITA It's just a slab laid over a ditch!

AGNES NITT Oh, I understand. It's some sort of test, is it? We're worried, so fear makes it a deep gorge. Perdita's always so confident, so she hardly notices it. Come on, we're wasting time! *(She steps on to the little slab of stone)* Rocks a bit, but it's all right, you just... (Suddenly her mind kicks in and it's a shaky bridge over a two hundred foot drop. She loses balance, falls but manages to hold on to the edge of the rickety bridge. All this is mimed; she stands as though*

*hanging from the bridge and looks up to talk to the others
as though they are above her)*

PERDITA You're standing in the water, you lump! All you have
to do is believe!

NANNY OGG Come on, girl! Give me your hand!

AGNES NITT Perdita tells me I'm standing in the stream, not
hanging over a two hundred foot drop!

NANNY OGG Do you think she's right?

AGNES NITT Don't know!

NANNY OGG She could be right, but gnarly ground can be
two things at the same time! Why don't you just let her
take over?

AGNES NITT I can't! She only does that when I'm really under
stress!

NANNY OGG Yes? And?

*The sound of rushing water is suddenly replaced by a
trickling sound as of a babbling brook. The strobe light
stops. A tight spotlight comes up on the* **WITCHES.**

PERDITA *pulls* **AGNES**'s *arms down to her sides.* **AGNES**
*snaps out of her delusion and looks down. She lifts her
feet as one would when finding oneself standing in a
shallow stream.*

AGNES NITT Damn.

NANNY OGG Right. Now on we go. But carefully, some of us
may have further to fall than others.

NANNY OGG *and* **MAGRAT GARLICK** *cross the stream
during the following.*

How's young Esme doing?

MAGRAT GARLICK Fine, Nanny.

NANNY OGG We've got to look after her.

By now they have all traversed the stream.

There. See? It really does change to suit your mood. It can be really high if you're in a bad mood.

AGNES NITT I wonder how high it was for Granny, then? Look, surely this isn't safe for the baby?

MAGRAT GARLICK It doesn't feel unsafe. Granny's here somewhere.

NANNY OGG That's right. Really close.

AGNES NITT How much further?

NANNY OGG Well, technic'ly just a few inches. There! *(She points)*

There is a loud flash and the onstage curtains open, revealing a cave. The lights cross fade. **GRANNY** *is in the cave, sitting on a rock, seemingly asleep. She holds a card that reads "GOE AWAY" and her box is nearby, as are an apple, water bottle and sandwich.*

Don't worry, she won't harm the baby. Couldn't do it. Hasn't got it in her.

NANNY OGG, AGNES NITT *and* **MAGRAT GARLICK** *move to* **GRANNY WEATHERWAX.**

The sound of the wind is replaced by that of dripping water.

(taking the card; reading) "GOE AWAY"? That's not very helpful.

AGNES NITT Can we wake her?

NANNY OGG Dangerous unless she's ready to come. *(She rootles about the cave)* Wrinkly apple, bottle of water and a cheese sandwich. And her box. *(She makes to open the box)*

AGNES NITT Should you do that?

GRANNY *stirs.*

NANNY OGG Thought opening her box would do it.

GRANNY WEATHERWAX Oh, it's you three. Why've you come?

AGNES NITT We thought you wanted us to.

GRANNY WEATHERWAX Three witches? No reason why not, I suppose. The maiden, the mother and—

NANNY OGG Go carefully.

GRANNY WEATHERWAX —the other one. Well, I expect you've got some dancin' to be doin', so I'll bid you good day.

NANNY OGG You know there're vampires in Lancre?

GRANNY WEATHERWAX Yes. *They* got invited!

NANNY OGG You know they're takin' over?

GRANNY WEATHERWAX Yes.

AGNES NITT So why did you run away up here?

GRANNY WEATHERWAX I can go where I like.

AGNES NITT Yes, but you ought—

GRANNY WEATHERWAX Oh, ought, is it? Where does it say I ought? There's lots of things I ought, I dare say.

NANNY OGG You know a magpie stole your invite?

GRANNY WEATHERWAX *(after a pause; she didn't know)* Yes. Course I did. Worked that out first thing.

NANNY OGG And you know young Verence got an Omnian priest to do the naming of young Esme?

GRANNY WEATHERWAX *(after another brief pause)* You know I put my mind to business. She looks comfortable.

PERDITA She didn't know the baby's name! I told you! Nanny thinks Granny's been in the baby's mind but if she was then she'd know the baby's name. She wouldn't do anything that'd hurt a child...

GRANNY WEATHERWAX Anyway, if there's a problem, you've got your three witches. You sort it out.

MAGRAT GARLICK You're going to hide up here?

GRANNY WEATHERWAX People aren't going to tell me what to do any more. Your husband invited vampires in and they don't have no power less'n you invite them in. Now they've got their teeth into the whole country. And I'm an old woman living in the woods and I've got to make it all better? I've had a lifetime of "ought" from "can" to "can't" and now it's over and I'll thank you for getting out of my cave. And that's an end to it.

There is a pause.

NANNY OGG Come on then. If we get a wiggle on we can be back before dark.

MAGRAT GARLICK Is that all?

GRANNY WEATHERWAX Things come to an end. I'm going to rest up here, then I'll move on. Plenty of places to go.

PERDITA Now get her to tell you the truth.

NANNY OGG Come on.

AGNES NITT But—

NANNY OGG No buts. Come on.

NANNY OGG, AGNES NITT, PERDITA and MAGRAT GARLICK move away from the cave. PERDITA is counting on her fingers.

The sound of the wind replaces that of dripping water and the lights cross-fade downstage.

Suddenly, NANNY stops and pats theatrically at her pockets.

Blow, I left me pipe back there.

PERDITA Five seconds.

NANNY OGG *darts back to the cave.*

MAGRAT GARLICK *and* **AGNES NITT** *move downstage to talk.*

AGNES NITT Granny was certainly not telling the truth.

MAGRAT GARLICK Of course she wasn't. She never does. She expects you to work it out for yourselves.

AGNES NITT She's right about the three witches, though.

MAGRAT GARLICK I never intended to come back to it, though. Perhaps when Esme's older a bit of aromatherapy, but not full time.

PERDITA And what have we got? The Knowing but Technically Inexperienced Young Woman, the Harrassed Young Mother and the Silver-Haired Golden-Ager! Doesn't exactly sound mythic, does it?

AGNES NITT Listen!

The lights cross-fade to the cave. The sound of dripping water replaces wind noise again.

NANNY OGG So – apart from that, how're you feelin'?

Silence.

The namin' went off all right.

GRANNY WEATHERWAX I can't beat 'em, Gytha, and that's a fact. They've got minds like steel. I can't touch them. I been tryin' every trick I've got! They've been searchin' for me but they can't focus right when I'm in here. The best one nearly got me at the cottage. My cottage! I've never felt anything like it, Gytha. He's had hundreds of years to get good. See them magpies all over Lancre? He uses them as eyes. They haven't found me here, yet. And he's clever, too. He's not going to fall for a garlic sandwich, that one. These vampires has learned. I can't find a way into them anywhere. They're more powerful, they're stronger, they think quicker. Going mind to mind with him's like spittin' at a thunderstorm.

NANNY OGG So what're you going to do?

GRANNY WEATHERWAX Nothing! There's nothing I can do! Don't you understand? Don't you know why I've been up here all day tryin'to think of something? They know all about magic. Borrowing's second nature to them. They think we're like cattle that can talk. There's no way round them.

NANNY OGG There's always away, Esme.

GRANNY WEATHERWAX I can't see it.

NANNY OGG You'll find a way. Weatherwaxes don't let themselves get beaten. It's like something in the blood, like I've always said.

GRANNY WEATHERWAX I am beaten. Even before I start. I'm up against a mind that's stronger than mine. I just about keep it away from me but I can't get in. I can't fight back.

NANNY OGG I never thought to hear you say that.

GRANNY WEATHERWAX Off you go. No point keepin' the baby hanging around in this cold.

NANNY OGG *moves back to* **AGNES NITT** *and* **MAGRAT GARLICK***. The lights cross-fade downstage. The sound of the wind replaces the sound of dripping water once more.*

AGNES NITT Got your pipe, then?

NANNY OGG Yes, thank you.

AGNES NITT What's she going to do?

NANNY OGG You tell me. I knows you was listenin'.

AGNES NITT If she's beaten, so are we, aren't we?

MAGRAT GARLICK What did she mean when she said "from can to can't"?

NANNY OGG Oh, from first thing in the mornin' when you can see, 'til last thing at night when you can't. *(She is suddenly* *positive)* Right. There's three of us. So we'll start by havin' a proper coven meeting.

AGNES NITT Aren't you worried? She's – giving up...

NANNY OGG Then it's up to us to carry on, isn't it? Back to my place, I think.

The wind sounds fade.

Blackout.

Scene Fifteen
Nanny Ogg's Cottage

There are a table and four chairs upstage. On the table is a cauldron.

The lights come up.

NANNY OGG *is directing* **MAGRAT GARLICK** *and* **AGNES NITT** *in their efforts to move the table further downstage.* (**PERDITA** *is present, too*).

NANNY OGG That's it, my girl, oh, and your majesty. Now, if we just put the cauldron in here, we'll have room for a proper coven.

MAGRAT GARLICK It doesn't feel right, having an indoor coven.

AGNES NITT It doesn't feel right, having a coven without Granny Weatherwax.

NANNY OGG
AGNES NITT } *(together)* True.
MAGRAT GARLICK

They set the table and cauldron down, then bring the chairs downstage and sit. **MAGRAT** *gets up again.*

MAGRAT GARLICK I'll make the tea, shall I?

NANNY OGG No, you sit down. It's Agnes's job to make the tea. You're the mother now, so it's your job to pour the tea.

AGNES NITT What's your job, Nanny?

NANNY OGG I drinks it.

AGNES NITT *exits.*

Right. We've got to find out more about these vampires while they're still actin' friendly. *(Calling offstage)* Agnes, you go back to the castle with Magrat and the baby.

AGNES NITT *(offstage)* What good will that do?

NANNY OGG Vampires don't affect you. As soon as they try to see Agnes's mind it sinks down and up pops Perdita. Just when they're looking at Perdita, here comes Agnes again. Young Vlad's definitely got his eye on you, eh?

AGNES NITT *puts her head round the door.*

AGNES NITT Certainly not!

AGNES NITT *disappears again.*

NANNY OGG Yeah, right. Men always like women who've got a bit of myst'ry about 'em. And while he's got his eye on you keepin' your eye on Magrat, you've got your other eye on him, understand? Everyone has a weakness. There's got to be a way.

AGNES NITT And if there isn't?

NANNY OGG You'll have to marry him.

A loud clatter of crockery, offstage.

MAGRAT GARLICK That's horrible!

AGNES NITT *enters with the tea things.*

AGNES NITT I'd rather kill myself!

PERDITA In the morning.

NANNY OGG Dun't have to be a long marriage. Put a pointy stake in your garter and our lad'll be getting cold even before they've finished cuttin' up the wedding cake.

AGNES NITT Nanny!

NANNY OGG Or maybe you could just sort of – make him change his ways a bit. It's amazin' what a wife can do if she knows her own mind. Or minds in your case, of course. F'rinstance – I was only married a month to the first Mr Ogg and already he was gettin' out of the bath if he needed to pee. S'easy to refine an 'usband.

AGNES NITT You have no scruples, Nanny.

NANNY OGG No. This is Lancre we're talkin' about. I ain't askin' her to do what I wouldn't do. If I was fifty years younger.

MAGRAT GARLICK You mean just because she's a woman she's got to use her sexual wiles on him? That is so... So... Well, it's so Nanny Ogg, that's all I can say.

NANNY OGG She can use what wiles she likes. I don't care what Granny says, there's always a way.

AGNES NITT You don't know what he's like. He looks at me as though he's undressing me with his eyes.

NANNY OGG Eyes is allowed.

AGNES NITT And he's laughing at me all the time! As if he knows I don't like him and that adds to the fun!

NANNY OGG Now look! You get into that castle! For Lancre! For the king! For everyone in the country! And if he gets too much, then let Perdita take over, 'cos I reckon there's some things she's better at!

AGNES NITT You can't treat people like this.

NANNY OGG I can. I'm the other one now, see?

Pause.

MAGRAT GARLICK Just like the old days. Arguing all the time.

AGNES NITT Nanny. You don't think Granny's doing this on purpose, do you? Keeping back, I mean, so that we have to form a three and work together?

NANNY OGG Why'd she do that?

MAGRAT GARLICK So that we'd develop insights and pull together and learn valuable lessons.

NANNY OGG She wouldn't think like that because that's soppy garbage. No, we got things Granny ain't got. *(She leans over and bangs on the wall of the cottage)*

AGNES NITT Such as what?

NANNY OGG Magrat's got a baby. I've got no scruples. And we've both got you. And you're in two minds about everything and that's good with vampires. We'll all go back to the castle. On our terms. Face down this count. And we'll take garlic and lemons and all the other stuff. And some of Mr Oats's holy water. You can't tell me all that stuff together won't work.

AGNES NITT And they'll let us in, will they?

NANNY OGG They'll have a lot to think about with that huge mob at the gates.

AGNES NITT What mob?

NANNY OGG There's seventy-nine Oggs in these parts.

> **JASON OGG** *enters.*

JASON OGG You knocked, Mum?

NANNY OGG There's goin' to be a spontaneous mob stormin' the castle in, oh, half an hour. Put the word out.

JASON OGG Yes, Mum.

NANNY OGG Tell ev'ryone I said it ain't compulsory for them to be there, of course.

JASON OGG Oh. Right. Is it flaming torches or scythes and stuff?

NANNY OGG Both, I think.

JASON OGG Battering ram?

NANNY OGG No. Shouldn't think so.

MAGRAT GARLICK Good. It is my front door, after all!

JASON OGG Anything special for people to shout, Mum?

NANNY OGG Just general shoutin', I think. Hop to it, then.

JASON OGG Yes, Mum.

> **JASON OGG** *exits.*

NANNY OGG Right. Now, you can leave young Esme next door with our Jason's wife...

MAGRAT GARLICK I'm keeping her with me.

AGNES NITT You can't do that!

MAGRAT GARLICK Don't you dare argue with me, Agnes Nitt!
Nor you, neither, Nanny.

NANNY OGG Wouldn't dream of it. Let's get the stuff together.
We're a coven, ladies. We're a trio. I miss Granny Weatherwax
as much as you do, but we've got to deal with things as she
would. *(She takes a deep breath)* I can't be having with this.

AGNES NITT It sounds better when she says it.

NANNY OGG I know.

The **WITCHES** *pick the table up and head upstage with it.*

Blackout.

Scene Sixteen
Mightily Oats's Tent

There is the sound of the wind.

OATS *sits at a table, reading by candlelight.*

We hear some of OAT*'s thoughts over the speakers.*

OATS'S VOICE This is useless! I didn't come here to be a vampire expert! "Ungodly Creatures" was a one hour lecture from deaf Deacon Thrope every fortnight. It didn't even count toward the final exam score!

OATS *(reading)* "The blood is the life... Vampires are subservient to the one who turns them into a vampire... As many as possible will drink from a victim so that he becomes a slave to all. Vampires can control bats, rats, weather... Contrary to legend, most victims merely become passive – not vampires. Intended vampire suffers terrible craving for blood... Garlic... Holy icons... Socks. Kill a vampire and you release all its victims.

OATS'S VOICE Why didn't anyone tell us that this stuff was important? Four years at theological college and I still don't know what I actually believe in. Mind you, the Church of Om schisms so often that the entire curriculum changed in the space of one afternoon. If you don't know what's true, how can you tell what to believe? I mean, it's not that I lack faith. But faith isn't enough. What I really need is knowledge.

OATS Right now, though, I'd settle for a reliable manual on vampire disposal. *(He sighs and returns to his book)*

The wind sounds fade.

Blackout

Scene Seventeen
Lancre Castle

There is the noise, offstage, of a large and rowdy mob.

AGNES NITT *enters surreptitiously with* **PERDITA**.

AGNES NITT *(speaking to the offstage* **NANNY OGG**, *sotto voce)*
I'll be all right, Nanny. Don't worry. I've got the holy water.

AGNES *crosses the stage and exits. Almost immediately,*
she is propelled back on to the stage by two **VAMPIRES**,
DEMONE *and* **KRIMSON**.

KRIMSON Well, well, well. Why are you in such a hurry, girl?

AGNES NITT Look, I'm very busy, so can we just speed this up?
Can we dispense with the "I like a girl with spirit" stuff?
Perhaps we could cut straight to the bit where I twist out
of your grip and kick you where it hurts.

DEMONE *punches* **AGNES NITT** *in the kidneys and she*
falls to her knees.

DEMONE I think not.

AGNES NITT
PERDITA } *(together)* I'll tell Vlad of you!

AGNES NITT Hah! Yes, he knows me!

PERDITA Hah!

KRIMSON What – you?

VLAD *enters.*

VLAD Yes. Her. Demone? Krimson? To me, please.

DEMONE *and* **KRIMSON** *reluctantly set off across the*
stage towards **VLAD**. **VLAD** *holds out his arm and*
DEMONE *and* **KRIMSON** *react as though skewered with*
hot wires. Both fall to the ground and twitch for a second
or two before going still.

That is the sort of thing we do not do to our guests. *(He moves to* **AGNES NITT***)* Did they hurt you? Just say the word and I'll turn what's left of them over to Lacrimosa.

PERDITA Say the word. At least there'd be two less of them.

AGNES NITT Er – no, thank you.

PERDITA Huh. Moral cowardice from the fat girl.

AGNES NITT Are they relatives of yours?

PERDITA Granny Weatherwax would have said yes.

VLAD Relatives – by blood, yes. In a way. But subservient. *(To* **DEMONE** *and* **KRIMSON***)* You two – get out.

DEMONE *and* **KRIMSON** *help each other offstage.*

AGNES NITT You mean vampirism is like pyramid selling?

VLAD Sorry? Selling pyramids?

AGNES NITT I mean, you bite five necks and in two months' time you get a lake of blood of your very own.

VLAD I can see we have a lot to learn.

IGOR *enters, carrying a grubby bucket.*

Igor!

IGOR Yeth, marthter?

VLAD You're putting down dust again, aren't you? Why are you putting down dust again?

IGOR You've got to have dutht, marthter. It'th tradithion.

VLAD Igor, Mother told you, we don't want dust. We don't want eyeholes cut into all the pictures and we certainly don't want your stupid box of trained spiders!

IGOR Thpider'th webth are what people ekthpect, marthter.

VLAD We don't want them!

IGOR The old ount liked them.

VLAD Just go away, will you!

IGOR *heads for the exit.*

And stand up straight and walk properly!

IGOR *reaches the exit.*

No one's impressed by the limp!

IGOR *exits.*

(to **AGNES NITT***)* I'm sorry you had to see that.

AGNES NITT Yes, I think I'm sorry, too.

VLAD He's going to be replaced. *(He notices the "fourth wall")* Ah, they've put the pictures up. Allow me to introduce the family. My great-uncle, the last – incumbent. He built our family home. Don'tgonearthe Castle, we call it.

AGNES NITT Strange name.

VLAD He used to laugh about it. The local coachmen used to warn vistors, you see. "Don't go near the castle", they'd say. "Even if it means spending the night up a tree, never go up there to the castle", they'd tell people. He said it was marvellous publicity. Sometimes he had every room full by nine p.m. and people would still be hammering on the door to get in. We won't see his like again. Rose from the dead so often his coffin had a revolving lid.

They look at the next "picture".

Ah, Aunt Carmilla. It was said she used to bathe in the blood of up to two hundred virgins at a time. I don't believe it, myself. Lacrimosa says if you use more than eighty, even a large bath will start to overflow.

AGNES NITT And, of course, it's so hard to find the soap.

VLAD Killed by a mob, I'm afraid.

AGNES NITT People can be so ungrateful.

On to the next "picture".

VLAD And this – was my grandfather.

AGNES NITT They all look very – powerful.

VLAD Yes. Powerful but dumb. Father thinks stupidity is somehow built into vampirism. As if the lust for fresh blood is linked to being as thick as a plank. Father is different.

AGNES NITT Different?

VLAD He recognises the need for family values. Most vampires don't. Humans are raising their successors, do you see, but we live for a very long time, so a vampire is raising competitors. He's trained us over the years to overcome our reaction to all the things that most vampires cannot bear. Garlic, religious symbols, daylight... We had to go out and play in daylight, I remember. And my nursery wallpaper was a mass of holy symbols. *(He sighs, in fond recollection)* That which does not kill us, he'd say, can only make us stronger...

AGNES NITT What about holy water ? *(She suddenly whips out a bottle of holy water and throws some over* **VLAD***)*

VLAD *(throwing his arms out, looking down at his chest and screaming)* Look at this waistcoat! Do you know what water does to silk? Do you? It's ruined! No matter what you do, there'll always be a mark! *(He smiles)* My dear Miss Nitt, it may just be a little more trouble than it's worth trying to get rid of us, do you see? I mean, what are we doing? Are we ravaging the country? No. Forcing our way into bedrooms? Certainly not. What's a little blood, for the good of the community? Of course, Verence will have to be demoted, but that won't be much of a loss, will it? And – our friends may find us grateful. What is the point of resisting?

AGNES NITT Are vampires ever grateful?

VLAD We could learn.

The **COUNT** *enters silently.*

AGNES NITT You're just saying that in exchange for not being evil, you'll merely be bad, is that it?

COUNT What we are saying, my dear, is that our time has come. Playing with your food, Vlad? Good evening, Miss Nitt. We appear to have a mob at the gates, Vlad.

VLAD Really? How exciting. I've never seen a real mob.

COUNT I wish your first could have been a better one. There's no passion in it. Still, it'd be tiresome if it goes on all through dinner. I shall tell them to go away.

The COUNT *and* VLAD *exit.*

A moment.

NANNY OGG *and* **MAGRAT GARLICK** *rush on.*

NANNY OGG Where are they?

AGNES NITT They've gone to look at the mob. But there's other vampires here, too.

MAGRAT GARLICK How many?

AGNES NITT I haven't found out, yet. *(She clears her throat)* Um, Vlad is trying to get to know me better!

NANNY OGG Good plan. See if he talks in his sleep.

AGNES NITT Nanny!

NANNY OGG Let's see his countship in action, shall we? We should get a view through the arrow squint in the gatehouse.

MAGRAT GARLICK I want to find Verence.

NANNY OGG He's not going anywhere. And I don't reckon they're planning to kill him.

AGNES NITT These are new vampires, Nanny. Not like the old sort.

NANNY OGG Then we face them down here and now. That's what Esme would do.

AGNES NITT But are we strong enough?

PERDITA Granny wouldn't have asked!

NANNY OGG There's three of us, isn't there? Come on.

They all exit.

Blackout.

Scene Eighteen
The Balcony Of Lancre Castle

A mob enters. This includes JASON, WAYNETTA, BERYL *and* DUANE OGG.

The COUNT *enters on to the balcony and talks to the mob below.*

COUNT Good evening. You must be the mob.

There are murmurs from the mob along the lines of "S'right, your grace", "Yeh, too right", "Yes, we is, as a matter of fact", etc.

The pitchforks are good. I like the pitchforks. And the blazing torches. The scythes, though. Not a good mob weapon. Start waving those around and someone's going to lose an ear. Do try to learn. What's your name? You at the front?

JASON OGG Er – Ogg, sir. Jason Ogg.

COUNT The blacksmith?

JASON OGG Yessir.

COUNT Wife and family doing well?

JASON OGG Yessir.

COUNT Well done. Got everything you need?

JASON OGG Er – yessir.

COUNT Good man. Carry on. If you could keep the noise down over dinner, I would be grateful, though I appreciate you have a traditional role to play. I'll have the servants bring out some mugs of hot toddy shortly. Oh, and may I introduce you to Sergeant Kraput.

SERGEANT KRAPUT *enters to the* COUNT's *right.* CORPORAL SVITZ *enters to his left.*

Known to his friends as "Bent Bill", I believe? And the other gentleman is Corporal Svitz, who has no friends at all. They and their men, who I suppose could be called soldiers in a sort of informal, easy come easy go, cut and thrust sort of way, will be going on duty in, oh, about an hour. Purely for reasons of security, you know.

CORPORAL SVITZ And then we'll gut yer like a clam and stuff yer with straw.

COUNT Ah. This is technical military language of which I know little. I do so hope there is no unpleasantness.

SERGEANT KRAPUT I don't.

COUNT What scamps they are. Good evening to you all. Thank you, gentlemen.

The COUNT, SERGEANT KRAPUT *and* CORPORAL SVITZ *exit.*

A moment's pause.

WAYNETTA OGG *(clearing her throat)* Right. Er. Well, Jason. I think we've made our point, don't you?

There are murmurings of welcome agreement from the rest of the mob.

BERYL OGG I think he knows our views.

More murmurs of agreement.

DUANE OGG Probably about time to open up. Anyone for a pint?

There is enthusiastic agreement. The mob drifts rapidly off.

JASON OGG *(as he leaves)* I suppose it's OK. Mum didn't say how long we was to stay. I s'pose.

Blackout.

Scene Nineteen
A Hall In Lancre Castle

The COUNT *walks on, followed by* VLAD, SERGEANT KRAPUT *and* CORPORAL SVITZ. NANNY OGG, AGNES NITT, PERDITA *and* MAGRAT *enter silently behind them.*

COUNT Ta-da! And that is how we do it!

NANNY OGG And d'you think you could do it twice?

COUNT *(waving away the two soldiers)* Ah, Mrs Ogg. And Agnes. Your Majesty. Now – was it three for a girl. Or three for a funeral? *(He moves to the* WITCHES*)*

OATS *enters on to the balcony and creeps along it during the following; when he gets to the opposite end he exits (and heads to stage level).*

No one except PERDITA *sees* OATS.

Do you think I'm stupid, dear ladies? Do you really think I'd let you run around if there was the least chance you could harm us?

There is a flash of lightning and a crash of thunder.

I can control the weather. And lesser creatures which, let me tell you, includes humans and yet you plot away and think you can have some kind of...of duel? However... *(He holds out an arm, his fingers straight and splayed)*

During the following, the WITCHES *rise on to their toes as if lifted and teeter backwards until they are against the wall. Once they are there, the* COUNT *lowers his arm but they remain transfixed.*

MAGRAT GARLICK *(as they move, in a strained voice)* What happened to us harnessing the power of all three of us?

NANNY OGG *(in an equally strained voice)* I rather depended on him standing still!

COUNT *(smiling)* Isn't anyone going to say "You won't get away with it?"

OATS *(shouting, offstage)* You won't get away with this!

COUNT And I didn't even see your lips move.

OATS *enters at stage level reading from a large book.*

The COUNT *turns to look at* OATS.

OATS *(reading)* "Depart from here and return to the grave from which thou came'st, unrighteous servant!"

NANNY OGG *(still held against the wall by the* COUNT's *power)* Where the hell did he come from?

PERDITA He was creeping along the minstrel gallery. You people see nothing!

OATS Er... "Get thee hence, thou worm of... "Erm— *(He consults the book)*

COUNT Excuse me?

OATS *(reading)* "—thou worm of Rheum. Thou spirit that troubles me..."

COUNT Could I just make a point?

OATS *(reading)* "Trouble not more the..." *(He looks up)* What?

COUNT *(taking the book from* OATS*)* Ossory's "Malleus Malificarum". Of course it has no effect, I helped to write it, you silly little man!

OATS But that was hundreds of years ago.

COUNT None of these work on vampires, didn't you even know that? Oh, I remember your prophets – they were men of passion! They didn't have little minds full of doubt and fretfulness. They were real priests, full of fire and bile! You are a joke! *(He throws away the book and takes* OATS's *religious pendant)* And this is the holy turtle of Om, which should make me cringe with fear? Not even a very good replica.

OATS And how would you know, foul fiend?

COUNT *(with a sigh)* No, no, that's for demons. Good effort, though. Well done. If ever I feel the need for a cup of tea and a bun, or possibly a cheery sing-song, I will give you a call. But in the meantime, you are in my way.

With minimal effort, the **COUNT** *sweeps* **OATS** *aside.* **OATS** *flies across the stage and falls to the ground.*

So much for piety. All that remains now is for Granny Weatherwax to turn up. It should be any minute now. After all, did you really think she'd trust you to get it right?

GRANNY WEATHERWAX *bursts in. She looks worn out and battered.*

Mistress Weatherwax! So good of you to come. Such a long walk on a dark night. Do sit by the fire a while and rest.

GRANNY WEATHERWAX I'll not rest here. You know well why I've come.

PERDITA She looks small. And tired.

COUNT Ah yes. The set-piece battle. The Weatherwax trademark. And, let me see, today your shopping list will be: "If I win I will expect you to free everyone and return to Überwald", right?

GRANNY WEATHERWAX No. I will expect you to die. *(She sways slightly)*

COUNT Excellent! But I know how you think, Mistress Weatherwax. You always have more than one plan. You're standing there, clearly one step away from collapse and yet... I'm not entirely certain I believe what I see.

GRANNY WEATHERWAX I couldn't give a damn what you're certain of. But you daren't let me walk out of here, I do know that. 'Cos you can't be sure of where I'll go, or what I'll do. I could be watching you from any pair of eyes. I might be behind any door. I could come from any direction, at any time.

VLAD *moves round, nearer to the three trapped* WITCHES.

And I'm good at malice.

COUNT   So? If I were impolite I could kill you right now. A simple arrow would do. Corporal Svitz?

SVITZ *raises his crossbow.*

GRANNY WEATHERWAX   Are you sure? Sure he'd have time for a second shot? Sure I'd still be here?

COUNT   You're not a shape-changer and you're in no condition to run.

VLAD   *(looking hard at* NANNY OGG*)* She's talking about moving herself into someone else's head.

NANNY OGG   Sorry, Esme, I couldn't stop meself thinking it.

COUNT   Ah yes. The famous Borrowing trick.

GRANNY WEATHERWAX   *(wearily)* But you don't know where. You don't know how far.

COUNT   So you put yourself elsewhere. So what?

GRANNY *makes a small gesture with her hand. The lights flicker. The* COUNT *flinches and the three trapped* WITCHES *fall to the ground, freed from the* COUNT'*s spell.*

Well done. A shot across my bows. I felt that. I actually felt it. No one in Überwald has ever managed to get through.

GRANNY WEATHERWAX   I can do better'n that.

COUNT   I don't think you can. If you could, you would have done so. No mercy for the vampire, eh? *(He approaches* GRANNY WEATHERWAX*)* Do you really think we're some form of gormless humans that can be cowed by a firm manner and a bit of trickery? I have tried to be understanding towards you, Mistress Weatherwax, because really we have a lot in common, but now...

GRANNY *gestures again. The lights flicker.*

(after a momentary pause) Oh dear, I hardly felt that one. Was that your best? Not good enough. Not nearly good enough.

The COUNT *gestures.* GRANNY WEATHERWAX *rises on her toes and backs away rapidly until she slams into the wall. She remains there, held by an invisible force, during the following.*

Don't think of it as losing, Granny Weatherwax. You will live forever. I would call that a bargain, wouldn't you?

GRANNY WEATHERWAX *(with a very strained voice)* I'd call that unambitious.

There is a loud and bright explosion. GRANNY *falls to the ground. The* VAMPIRES *look surprised.*

NANNY OGG She's gone. She's sent herself somewhere.

MAGRAT GARLICK Where?

NANNY OGG Don't think about it!

MAGRAT GARLICK *(with a gasp)* Oh no...

NANNY OGG Don't think it – don't think it! Pink elephants! Pink elephants!

MAGRAT GARLICK She wouldn't—

NANNY OGG *drags* MAGRAT GARLICK *toward the exit.*

NANNY OGG Lalalala! Ee-ei-ee-ei-oh! Come on, let's go! Over to you two, Agnes!

NANNY OGG *and* MAGRAT *exit, hurriedly.*

COUNT Igor! Where are you, you stupid—

IGOR *appears silently behind the* COUNT.

IGOR Yeth, marthter?

COUNT Why do you always turn up like that?

IGOR The old count alwayth exthpected it, marthter.

COUNT Well, stop it!

IGOR Yeth, marthter.

COUNT Take that... *(He indicates* GRANNY WEATHERWAX*)* and lay it on the dining table and then ring the dinner gong.

IGOR *drags* GRANNY WEATHERWAX *offstage.*

(calling after IGOR*)* And I've told you before about that walk! *(He turns to* AGNES NITT*)* Miss Nitt? Would you like to stay for dinner?

AGNES NITT You're going to... You're going to suck her blood?

COUNT We are vampires. A little – sacrament, shall we say?

AGNES NITT But she's an old lady.

COUNT *(moving to* AGNES NITT*)* The idea of a younger aperitif is attractive, believe me, but Vlad would sulk. Anyway, blood develops character with age, like your old wines. She won't be killed. Not as such. At her time of life she should welcome a little immortality.

AGNES NITT But she hates vampires!

COUNT That could present her with a problem when she comes round since she will be a rather subservient one. Oh, and would you take him... *(He indicates the still unconscious* OATS*)* with you when you go?

AGNES NITT You won't be able to turn her into a vampire!

COUNT She won't be able to help it. It's in the blood, if we choose to put it there.

AGNES NITT She'll resist.

COUNT That could be worth seeing. Now go away, Miss Nitt. Take your soggy priest. After – dinner, well you can have your old witch back. But she'll be ours. *(Aside, to* **VLAD***)* Vlad, she followed you home, you may keep her, but she's your responsibility. You have to feed her and clean out her cage. *(Aloud, to* **AGNES NITT***)* Goodbye, Miss Nitt.

The **COUNT** *exits.* **VLAD** *crosses to* **AGNES NITT.**

VLAD Shall I see you again tomorrow?

AGNES NITT *glares at* **VLAD.**

VLAD *exits after the* **COUNT.**

AGNES NITT *helps* **OATS** *to his feet.*

OATS Oh, that poor old woman.

AGNES NITT When she... When she disappeared, I felt her voice in my head. She said "Leave me". We all felt her set her mind free.

OATS But where has it gone?

AGNES NITT Well, the baby is called Esme, isn't it? That's what Nanny and Magrat think, but I reckon that it'd be too romantic, too folkloric a thing for Granny to have done. So, where is she? She's put the essence of herself somewhere for safety and despite what she told the Count it couldn't have been far away.

OATS If only I'd used the right exorcism...

AGNES NITT It wouldn't have worked, I don't think they're very religious vampires.

OATS A priest only gets a chance like this once in his life...

AGNES NITT You were just the wrong person. If a pamphlet had been the right thing to scare them away, you'd have been the best man for the job. *(She pauses and stares at him)*

PERDITA Are you thinking what I'm thinking?

OATS What are you looking at?

AGNES NITT Vampires don't affect your head, do they? They don't affect your mind? Can't tell what you're thinking?

OATS Half the time I can't tell what I'm thinking!

AGNES NITT Really?

PERDITA Really?

OATS I've let everyone down, haven't I? But I'm ready to have a second go.

AGNES NITT I'm not sure they'd let us go a second time. They let us go because it was cruel thing to do. Dang! They've left me to decide what to do now, and it shouldn't be me. I shouldn't have to decide things. What is it she wants me to do?

PERDITA Especially now you think you know where she's hiding.

AGNES NITT If a vampire wants to turn you into a vampire, what happens?

OATS I – think they put something in the blood. If they want to turn you into a vampire, you get turned. I don't think you can fight it once it's in the blood. You can't say you don't want to join.

AGNES NITT Granny's good at resisting.

OATS That good?

DEMONE *and* **KRIMSON** *carry on* **GRANNY WEATHERWAX.**

DEMONE Ah, Miss Nitt. Good, you haven't left. Here, you can take away the empties!

DEMONE *and* **KRIMSON** *dump* **GRANNY WEATHERWAX** *and then exit, laughing.*

AGNES NITT *and* **OATS** *move to* **GRANNY WEATHERWAX** *and pick her up.*

AGNES NITT They didn't even lock her up.

OATS They probably feel she already is locked up. Let's get her out of here.

AGNES NITT *and* OATS *carry* GRANNY WEATHERWAX *out.*

A moment.

NANNY OGG *and* MAGRAT GARLICK *enter from a different direction. They head across the stage during the following.*

NANNY OGG Right, now, my girl, let's get out of here while we can. I reckon our best bet is to walk out bold as brass.

MAGRAT GARLICK What about Verence? I can't just leave him!

NANNY OGG What will they do to him that you could prevent if you was here? Keep the baby safe, that's the important thing. It always has been. Now just follow me and act snooty. You must have learned that, bein' a queen.

KRIMSON *enters and blocks their way.*

Oh bugger.

KRIMSON Ladies. May I be of assistance?

MAGRAT GARLICK We were just leaving.

KRIMSON Possibly not.

NANNY OGG Excuse me, young vampire. But what part of Überwald are you from?

KRIMSON Klotz.

NANNY OGG Really? That's nice. (*She takes a piece of card from her pocket, read sit, then takes out a lemon*) Now what's the name of that river that runs through Klotz? The Um, is it? The Eh?

KRIMSON The Ah...

NANNY OGG *rams the lemon into* KRIMSON'*s mouth and bangs him/her on the top of the head, forcing him/her to bite into the lemon. He/she screams and falls to his/ her knees.*

NANNY OGG What a very strange superstition. Now then, we ought to cut off its head...

MAGRAT GARLICK Shall we just go? Before someone else comes?

NANNY *shoves* KRIMSON *off through a doorway and returns to* MAGRAT.

Almost immediately, IGOR *enters, muttering to himself.*

IGOR Thilly voithe? Thilly walk? What the hell do they know? Fetcth thith, fetcth that – never a morthel of rethpect. *(He sees* NANNY OGG*)*

NANNY OGG Ah, Mr Igor. We need a carriage out of here and you're going to help.

IGOR Yeth, mithtreth.

MAGRAT GARLICK What? As easy as that?

IGOR Yeth. I'm leaving anyway. Thith lot are a dithgrathe to the spethies! It'th a pleathure to be commanded in thuch a clear, authoratative voithe. Igor liketh to know where he thtandth.

MAGRAT GARLICK Slightly lopsidedly?

IGOR The old marthter uthed to whip me every day!

MAGRAT GARLICK You liked that?

IGOR Of corthe not. But it'th proper! He wath a gentleman, who'th bootth I wathn't fit to lick clean...

NANNY OGG But you did anyway?

IGOR Every morning. Uthed to get a lovely thine, too.

NANNY OGG Right, come on, Mr Igor. You're going to take us somewhere safe.

MAGRAT GARLICK Are you going to trust him?

NANNY OGG I'm a good judge of character, me. Always trust a man with stitches all round his head.

IGOR, *NANNY OGG* and *MAGRAT GARLICK head for the exit.*

The DE MAGPYRS *enter. They watch* IGOR, NANNY OGG *and* MAGRAT GARLICK.

IGOR, NANNY OGG *and* MAGRAT GARLICK *exit.*

The DE MAGPYRS *turn to the audience and stare at them.*

Blackout.

ACT II

Scene One
Agnes Nitt's Cottage

GRANNY WEATHERWAX *is lying, still, on a bed. Beside the bed kneels* **OATS**, *in prayer.* **AGNES NITT** *and* **PERDITA** *stand nearby.*

AGNES NITT Sorry? Did you say something?

OATS Just a short prayer. The Prophet Brutha says that Om helps those who help one another.

AGNES NITT And does he?

OATS To be honest, there are a number of opinions. About a hundred and sixty, in fact, since the schism of ten-thirty a.m., February the twenty-third. That was when the Re-United Free Chelonists (Hubwards Convocation) split from the Re-United Free Chelonists (Rimwards Convocation). It was rather serious.

AGNES NITT Blood spilled?

OATS No, but there were fisticuffs and a deacon had ink spilled on him.

AGNES NITT Goodness. Are you always arguing?

OATS The Prophet Brutha said "Let there be a thousand voices". Sometimes I think he meant it was better to argue amongst ourselves than go out putting unbelievers to fire and sword. The vampire was right, we've lost the fire.

AGNES NITT But they used to burn people with it.

OATS I know... I know.

Suddenly GRANNY WEATHERWAX *sits upright.*

Oh. And how are you, Miss Weatherwax?

AGNES NITT She was bitten by vampires! What sort of question is that?

OATS Well, it's better than "What are you?" I would think.

AGNES NITT *feels* GRANNY WEATHERWAX's *forehead.*

AGNES NITT She's burning up! Get some water!

OATS *exits.*

GRANNY WEATHERWAX *seems to be trying to speak.* AGNES NITT *leans down to her.* OATS *enters with a glass of water.*

OATS Here!

AGNES NITT She said something. "I am", I think.

GRANNY WEATHERWAX *(still indistinct)* Iron.

OATS Iron. I think she said "iron". What does she mean? Iron's no good against vampires.

AGNES NITT Iron! She needs something made of iron to focus on. To focus her pain. There's an anvil in the shed. I'll get it.

GRANNY WEATHERWAX *(with difficulty)* No! *(She points at* OATS*)* You go.

OATS *runs out.*

You must go where the others are. It'll need three witches if this goes wrong. You'll have to face – something terrible.

AGNES NITT What terrible thing?

GRANNY WEATHERWAX Me. Go. Go now!

AGNES NITT But what if...?

GRANNY WEATHERWAX Get away!

OATS *enters with an anvil and puts it down.*

AGNES NITT I have to go. Keep an eye on her!

AGNES NITT *exits.*

GRANNY WEATHERWAX Mr Priest, somewhere in this place is an axe. Find it and sharpen it.

OATS Er...

GRANNY WEATHERWAX Then find some wood and sharpen it to a point, and find a hammer...

OATS Madam, what are you wanting me to—

GRANNY WEATHERWAX I need to focus my mind. Something will get up presently. Make sure you know well what it is.

OATS You're not expecting me to behead—

GRANNY WEATHERWAX I'm commanding you, religious man! What do you really – believe? What did you think it was all about? Singing songs? Sooner or later, it's all down to blood. Go on, man. Do as you're told.

OATS *exits.*

GRANNY WEATHERWAX *moves to the anvil and kneels by it. She takes it in both hands. A strobe light comes on and there is a crackling sound; an eerie sound begins which continues throughout the following scene. The anvil starts to glow.* **GRANNY WEATHERWAX** *stares hard into the anvil.*

Right. This is a test. Everything is a test. Everything is a competition. You make choices. No one ever tells you which ones were right. Oh, some people say you get given points after death, but where's the point of that? Head's full of fog. Need to think. This – isn't a real place. No, that's not right. This isn't a usual place. It might be more real than Lancre.

DEATH *appears on the balcony.*

DEATH GOOD EVENING.

GRANNY WEATHERWAX Oh, you again? You are Death, I take it?

DEATH I AM. ANOTHER CHOICE, ESMERELDA WEATHERWAX.

GRANNY WEATHERWAX Light and dark? Black and white? It's never as simple as that, is it? Not even for you.

DEATH *(with a sigh)* NO. NOT EVEN FOR ME.

GRANNY WEATHERWAX Which light? Which dark? This doesn't feel right. It's not what I was expecting. Whose light? How do vampires think? Whose mind is this? Don't be stupid, Esme. It's my mind. I'm always me. Don't lose your grip on that, Esme. So, light in front of me, darkness behind...

(to DEATH*)* Am I dyin'?

DEATH YES.

GRANNY WEATHERWAX Will I die?

DEATH YES.

GRANNY WEATHERWAX But, hold on: from your point of view, everyone is dyin' and everyone will die, right?

DEATH YES.

GRANNY WEATHERWAX So you're not actually bein' a lot of help, are you?

DEATH I'M SORRY, I THOUGHT YOU WANTED THE TRUTH. PERHAPS YOU WERE EXPECTING JELLY AND ICE-CREAM.

GRANNY WEATHERWAX Hah! But I've talked to people who've nearly died. Sometimes they talked about seeing a light. But is the light the way in, or the way out?

DEATH CHOOSE. YOU ARE GOOD AT CHOOSING, I BELIEVE.

GRANNY WEATHERWAX Any advice you can give me?

DEATH CHOOSE RIGHT.

DEATH *exits and is replaced by another* GRANNY WEATHERWAX, *identically dressed and wigged but with a completely blacked-out face. The second* GRANNY WEATHERWAX's *dialogue is recorded.*

GRANNY'S VOICE Because of you, some died who may have lived...

GRANNY WEATHERWAX Some lived who would surely have died.

GRANNY'S VOICE You killed...

GRANNY WEATHERWAX No. I showed the way.

GRANNY'S VOICE That's just words. You took the right to judge others.

GRANNY WEATHERWAX I took the duty. I'll admit that.

GRANNY'S VOICE I know every evil thought you've ever had—

GRANNY WEATHERWAX I know.

GRANNY'S VOICE —the ones you'd never dare to tell anyone—

GRANNY WEATHERWAX I know.

GRANNY'S VOICE —all the little secrets never to be told—

GRANNY WEATHERWAX I know.

GRANNY'S VOICE —how often you longed to embrace the dark—

GRANNY WEATHERWAX Yes.

GRANNY'S VOICE —such strength you could have. Embrace the dark, Esme—

GRANNY WEATHERWAX No.

GRANNY'S VOICE Give in to me. Your sister Lilith did. Your mother Alison did—

GRANNY WEATHERWAX That's never been proved!

GRANNY'S VOICE Give in to me.

GRANNY WEATHERWAX No. I know you. I've always known you. The count just let you out to torment me, but I've always known who you are. I've fought you every day of my life and you'll get no victory now. I knows who you are now, Esmerelda Weatherwax. You don't scare me no more!

The eerie sound stops.

Blackout.

Scene Two
A Corridor In The Castle

AGNES NITT *enters with* PERDITA.

PERDITA Why are we back here?

AGNES NITT I need to get to Nanny. Granny sent us, me, away.

PERDITA Yes, commanded you. Even I felt its strength. Like a bucket of ice.

VLAD *enters.*

VLAD Why, Miss Nitt. Back again? If you're looking for Nanny Ogg, they "escaped" in our coach. Stole it, you know.

AGNES NITT They got away from you!

VLAD Oh, hardly. Father could easily have stopped the coach if he'd wanted. But we prefer the personal touch.

AGNES NITT The in-your-neck approach.

VLAD Yes, indeed. So can't I persuade you to become one of us, Agnes?

AGNES NITT What, someone who lives by taking life from other people?

VLAD We don't usually go as far as that, now. And when we do... Well, we only kill people who deserve to die.

AGNES NITT Oh, well that's all right then. I'm sure I'd trust a vampire's judgement.

VLAD My sister can be a little too – rigorous at times, I admit.

AGNES NITT I've seen the servants you brought with you. They're so passive, they almost moo.

VLAD Well? It's not much different to the lives they would have had, anyway. And at least they're well-fed, sheltered...

AGNES NITT Milked?

VLAD And is that bad? You've travelled, Agnes. You know that so many people lead little lives, always under the whip of some king or master who won't hesitate to sacrifice them in battle or turn them out of their homes when they can't work any more.

PERDITA But they can run away.

AGNES NITT But they can run away.

VLAD Really? With a family? No money? Most would never try. Most people put up with most things, Agnes.

AGNES NITT That's the most unpleasant, cynical—

PERDITA Accurate.

AGNES NITT —accurate – no!

VLAD You have a strange mind, Agnes. You are not one of these cattle. You witches know your own mind. I wish I did. Come. Father says we should make you all vampires. He says you're half-way there, anyway. But I'd rather you came to see how marvellous it could be.

AGNES NITT What? I'd like to constantly be craving blood?

VLAD You constantly crave chocolate, don't you?

AGNES NITT How dare you!

VLAD Blood tends to be low in carbohydrates. The pounds will just drop away—

AGNES NITT That's sickening!

VLAD You'll have complete control over yourself.

AGNES NITT I'm not listening.

VLAD All it takes is a little prick—

AGNES NITT It's not going to be yours, mister! Look, if you're going to bite me, just get on with it.

VLAD (*slipping momentarily into* **GRANNY**-*speak – the call of the blood*) Oh, I couldn't be 'aving with that.

VLAD *and* **AGNES NITT** *briefly look confused by this un-cool choice of language.*

AGNES NITT You did it to Granny.

VLAD Yes, but when it's against someone's will, they end up so compliant. You're far too interesting to be a slave.

LACRIMOSA *enters.*

LACRIMOSA Are you still toying with her? Bite her or let her go. Come on, Father wants you. He knows where they're going with the baby.

VLAD This is my affair, Lacci.

LACRIMOSA Every boy should have a hobby, but really!

VLAD Come on, Agnes.

PERDITA Granny did say you should be with the others.

AGNES NITT But how will I find them when we get there?

VLAD Oh, we'll find them.

AGNES NITT I meant—

VLAD Do come. We don't intend to hurt your friends—

LACRIMOSA Much.

PERDITA Anyway, if they're chasing them, you may as well go with them. And you'll get to fly – that'd be coo-ool!

LACRIMOSA I suppose you could attach a piece of string to her ankle and tow her around like a balloon.

VLAD Come on, Agnes.

VLAD *and* **LACRIMOSA** *exit.*

AGNES NITT Besides, if I go with them, there's always a chance that, at some point, I might find myself alone in a room with Lacrimosa. I wouldn't need garlic, or a stake, or an axe. Just five minutes alone.

PERDITA And perhaps a pin.

Blackout.

Scene Three
Back At Agnes's Cottage

There is a double-headed axe on the table.

Thunder and lightning.

GRANNY *is kneeling as before by the anvil.*

OATS *enters. He sees the axe and moves as if to pick it up.*

GRANNY WEATHERWAX *(standing, slowly)* You wouldn't reach it in time. You should've kept hold of it if you planned to use it. Prayer's all very well, but an axe is an axe no matter what you believes.

A moment's pause, as OATS *awaits his fate.*

(moving to OATS*)* If you've got any tea on the go I could murder a cup. I'm parched.

OATS Tea? Oh, right. Yes. Tea. *(He starts to sidle offstage)*

GRANNY WEATHERWAX A biscuit wouldn't come amiss.

OATS *makes a charge for the axe, but* GRANNY WEATHERWAX *is there first.*

Still too slow. *(She gives* OATS *the axe)* Keep hold of it, though. Axe first, pray later. Who is your god, anyway, Mr Priest?

OATS Om. Er – you don't mind, do you?

GRANNY WEATHERWAX Mind? Why should I mind?

OATS Well… Er, your, um, colleagues keep telling me that the Omnians used to burn witches.

GRANNY WEATHERWAX They never did.

OATS I'm afraid that the records do show—

GRANNY WEATHERWAX They never burned witches. Probably they burned some old ladies who spoke up or couldn't run away. I wouldn't look for witches bein' burned. I'd look for witches doin' the burnin', though. We ain't all nice. *(She smiles, not entirely a reassuring sight)* Now, where's that tea and biscuit, mm?

OATS *scuttles off.*

OATS *(offstage)* I want to be certain. Are you... Are you a vampire?

GRANNY WEATHERWAX Just you hurry up with that tea, Mr Priest.

OATS *enters with a cup of tea and a biscuit. He has left the axe in the wings.* GRANNY *takes the tea and has a long drink of it.*

Now that is better. Not bad tea, for an Omnian. Now we'll go up to the castle.

OATS What for? Why?

GRANNY WEATHERWAX Good grief man, why do you think?

OATS The vampires have gone. They went after the coach. Shawn and Jason Ogg and some others are outside. Jason said he saw Mrs Ogg driving it. There's just a few servants and guards left at the castle now.

GRANNY WEATHERWAX How're the vampires travellin', then? If Nanny's got their coach?

OATS Oh, they're flying, apparently. Shawn saw them disappearing off the castle roof. They had Agnes Nitt with them.

GRANNY WEATHERWAX Agnes will be all right. She's a sensible girl. So Nanny's got them away from the castle, eh? Now, where would she have taken them? *(To OATS)* Which way did they go?

OATS Jason didn't see. But can't you tell? I thought you could read minds or something?

GRANNY WEATHERWAX Right now, Mr Priest, I don't think I
can read my own mind, let alone Gytha Ogg's. But I know
how her mind works. She'll have taken them all to Überwald.

OATS Überwald? What makes you think that?

GRANNY WEATHERWAX Because nowhere in Lancre's safe, and
she wouldn't risk taking them up to the gnarly ground on
a night like this with the baby an' all.

OATS But Überwald? That's taking them straight into danger!

GRANNY WEATHERWAX More dangerous than here? They
know about vampires in Überwald. They're used to 'em.
There're safe places – buildings with thick stone walls.
Nanny's practical. She'll think of that. But they'll end up
at the vampires' castle.

OATS Surely not!

GRANNY WEATHERWAX I can feel it in my blood. That's the
trouble with Gytha Ogg. Far too practical.

There is a noise, off, from a small mob.

SHAWN OGG *and* JASON OGG *enter with some other
villagers, including* BESTIALITY CARTER.

Ah, a useful mob, Mr Priest. Just what we need. Shawn Ogg,
this priest says there are still guards at the castle?

SHAWN OGG They've locked themselves in the keep, mistress.
We can't get in. And they've got the king!

GRANNY WEATHERWAX But can they get out?

SHAWN OGG No, mistress. But the armoury's in there.

GRANNY WEATHERWAX I need a horse. Fetch one up here. I'll
be off to get the girls back.

OATS Into Überwald? Alone? I couldn't let you do that!

GRANNY WEATHERWAX I ain't asking you to let me do anything.
No off you go and get a horse.

OATS But you can hardly stand!

GRANNY WEATHERWAX Certainly I can.

OATS (*turning to* **JASON** *and* **SHAWN OGG**) You wouldn't let a poor old lady go off to confront monsters on a wild night like this, would you?

BESTIALITY CARTER So why should we care what happens to monsters?

SHAWN OGG That's Granny Weatherwax, that is.

OATS But she's an old lady!

The crowd, including **SHAWN** *and* **JASON OGG**, *gasp at this.* **SHAWN** *and* **JASON OGG** *step away from* **OATS** *slightly.*

Would you go out on a night like this?

BESTIALITY CARTER Depends if I knew where Granny Weatherwax was.

GRANNY WEATHERWAX Don't think I didn't hear that, Bestiality Carter. Now, Mr Oats. A horse!

OATS I've got a mule. It's at the stables.

GRANNY WEATHERWAX That'll do. Let's get it, then. You lot – off you go. I just need a quiet word with this priest.

JASON OGG But what about the king?

GRANNY WEATHERWAX He'll be safe enough for the time being – he's a useful hostage. You lot go and besiege the castle, though. It'll keep you and them occupied. Go on!

JASON and **SHAWN OGG** *and the mob exit.*

GRANNY and **OATS** *head for the same exit.*

Have they gone? Is there anyone watchin' me?

OATS Only me.

GRANNY WEATHERWAX You don't count. No offence. *(She collapses)*

OATS *supports* **GRANNY WEATHERWAX.**

Let go, let go! I just lost my footin'.

OATS Yes, yes, of course.

GRANNY WEATHERWAX And don't try to humour me, neither.

OATS No, of course not. But perhaps I'll just take your arm. It's quite muddy out there.

GRANNY WEATHERWAX Well, if you think you're going to fall over...

OATS Yes, that's right. I hurt my ankle on the way up here, slipping on some mud.

GRANNY WEATHERWAX I've always said young people today don't have any stamina.

OATS That's right. No stamina.

GRANNY WEATHERWAX And I expect your eyesight's none too good, with all that book-readin'?

OATS Blind as a bat. That's right.

GRANNY WEATHERWAX *(leaning on his arm)* Well, I'll help you along then.

They move along like this until they reach the exit.

OATS Look, why don't I come with you? To Überwald.

GRANNY WEATHERWAX You'd be a bit of a hindrance. I'd be worryin' about you all the time. *(She sags again)* Oh, well. If you insist. Just so long as you understand that I didn't ax you to come along and I don't need your help.

OATS Ax?

GRANNY WEATHERWAX Ask, then. Slipped into a bit of rural, there.

OATS Oh – "axe". Right.

> **OATS** *props* **GRANNY WEATHERWAX** *against the wall. He dashes off, picks up the axe, hammer and stake, and returns to* **GRANNY WEATHERWAX.**

GRANNY WEATHERWAX You're learnin'.

> **GRANNY WEATHERWAX** *leans on* **OATS** *again and they move purposefully off.*

> *Blackout.*

Scene Four
Atop A Mountain

There is the sound of the wind.

AGNES NITT, PERDITA *and* **VLAD** *are on stage.*

VLAD *(a little out of breath)* We'll – just take a break...here, if that's OK. Not much further now – Agnes.

AGNES NITT Are you all right? That was amazing. I thought you people turned into bats when you flew.

VLAD *(laughing)* Oh, we can if we want. But that's a bit too melodramatic for Father. *(He looks out and up and waves, as if to the passing* **COUNT***)* He says we shouldn't conform to stereotypes. *(He points offstage)* Look, there's Morbidia, except she's calling herself Tracy at the moment. *(He calls to her)* Morbidia! This is Agnes!

MORBIDIA *(offstage)* I saw you had freight on board, Vlad! Having a well-earned rest? Agnes, eh? What a well-chosen name!

AGNES NITT IT'S MY REAL ONE... OH, NEVER MIND.

PERDITA I bet she's not a natural brunette! And if I used that much mascara I'd at least try not to look like Harry the Happy Panda!

VLAD *(calling after* **MORBIDIA***)* We're all stopping off in Escrow. Father says we need a feed to break our journey. That old witch was barely a snack! See you there. *(To* **AGNES NITT***)* You'll like Escrow. It's a charming little town.

AGNES NITT You're going to feed there?

VLAD It's not what you think.

AGNES NITT You don't know what I think.

VLAD I can guess, though. People being dragged out of their beds, blood on the walls, that sort of thing? That's really most unfair, you know.

AGNES NITT You attacked Granny Weatherwax! You bit her!

VLAD Symbolically. We all did it, to welcome her into the family.

AGNES NITT And that makes it better, does it? And she'll be a vampire?

VLAD Certainly. A good one, too. But that's only horrifying if you think being a vampire is a bad thing. We don't. Yes, Escrow will be good for you. You'll see what can be done.

VLAD *"freezes" during the next exchange between* **AGNES** *and* **PERDITA**.

PERDITA He does smile nicely.

AGNES NITT He's a vampire!

PERDITA All right, but apart from that...

AGNES NITT Apart from that?

PERDITA Nanny would say, make the most of it.

AGNES NITT But can you imagine kissing that?

PERDITA Yes, I can.

AGNES NITT I will admit, he does smile nicely. And he's very smart.

PERDITA But have you noticed?

AGNES NITT Noticed what?

PERDITA He's – changed. There's something different about him. Something new...

VLAD *unfreezes.*

VLAD Father says Escrow is a model community. It shows what happens if you put ancient enmity aside and humans and vampires learn to live in peace. Escrow is the future.

They all head for the exit.

The wind sounds fade. Blackout.

Scene Five
On The Road To Überwald

Thunder, lightning and heavy rain.

GRANNY *and* OATS *enter.* OATS *is singing a hymn.*

GRANNY WEATHERWAX What is that you're singing?

OATS "Om is in His Holy Temple". It keeps my spirits up.

GRANNY WEATHERWAX Huh! We need it after your damn donkey went lame. So – you take comfort from it, do you?

OATS Yes.

GRANNY WEATHERWAX Even that bit about "crushing infidels"?

OATS Well, no. That line's not in the currently approved version. My gran taught me this one.

GRANNY WEATHERWAX Keen on crushing infidels, was she?

OATS Well, I think she was quite keen on crushing Mrs Ashram next door to be honest but, yes, she thought the world would be a better place with a bit more crushing and smiting.

GRANNY WEATHERWAX Prob'ly true.

OATS A bit judgemental, my gran.

GRANNY WEATHERWAX Nothing wrong with that. Judging is human. This and that, good and bad, judging, making choices every day – that's human.

OATS But how do you know you're making the right decisions?

GRANNY WEATHERWAX I just do the best I can. Mercy's a fine thing, but judgement comes first. Otherwise you don't know what you're bein' merciful about. Anyway, I thought you Omnians were still keen on smitin' and crushin'?

OATS Those were – different days. We use crushing arguments now.

GRANNY WEATHERWAX And long, pointed debates, I suppose?

OATS Well, there are two sides to every question...

GRANNY WEATHERWAX What do you do when one of them's wrong?

OATS Mistress Weatherwax, you are a natural disputant.

GRANNY WEATHERWAX No I ain't!

OATS You'd enjoy yourself at the Synod. They love a good argument. They've been known to argue for days about how many angels can dance on the head of a pin.

GRANNY WEATHERWAX Domestic pin? That'd be sixteen.

OATS You've counted?

GRANNY WEATHERWAX No. But it's as good an answer as you'll get. So that's what they discuss, is it?

OATS Yes, though there's a very interesting argument raging at the moment about the nature of sin.

GRANNY WEATHERWAX Right. Against it, are they?

OATS It's not as simple as that. It's not a black and white issue. There are so many shades of grey.

GRANNY WEATHERWAX No. There's no greys, only white that's got grubby. And sin, young man, is when you treat people as things. That's what sin is.

OATS It's a lot more complicated than that...

GRANNY WEATHERWAX No, it ain't. When people say that, it's 'cos they're gettin' worried that they won't like the truth. People as things. That's where it starts.

OATS I'm sure there are worse crimes...

GRANNY WEATHERWAX But they starts with thinking about people as things. Strong in your faith, are you?

OATS I try to be.

GRANNY WEATHERWAX But why, Mr Oats? Why do you have faith?

OATS If I didn't, I wouldn't have anything.

GRANNY WEATHERWAX But you read a lot of books. Hard to have faith, isn't it, when you read a lot of books?

OATS Yes. You're not a believer yourself then, Mistress Weatherwax?

GRANNY WEATHERWAX Oh, I reckon I believes in tea, sunrises, that sort of thing.

> **GRANNY WEATHERWAX** *stumbles and falls against* **OATS**.

OATS Are you all right?

GRANNY WEATHERWAX It's not far now! Oh, I've been so stupid... *(She collapses to the ground)*

> **OATS** *kneels by* **GRANNY WEATHERWAX** *and feels her pulse.*

OATS *(to himself)* Very weak. *(He pats her face gently)*

GRANNY WEATHERWAX *(weakly)* If you mention religion at this point, I'll give you such a hidin'...

OATS You're so cold. It's as though you push warmth away from you. *(He removes his cloak and drapes it over* **GRANNY WEATHERWAX***)* Fire, that's what we need. Fire brings life and drives away the darkness. Everything round here's so wet. There's nothing that'll burn. "Whenever you are in a dilemma, young Oats, rely on the Book of Om for guidance"... *(He pulls out the Book of Om and allows it fall open at random. With his eyes shut he selects a passage. Then, reading)* "...And Brutha looked upon Gul-Arah, and the lamentation of the desert, and rode him then on to..." No help there. *(He closes the book and allows it fall open again. Again, eyes shut, he selects a passge to read. Reading)* "And in that time, in the land of the Cyrinites, there was a multiplication of camels." Om, help me. Help us. She is not of our faith but she needs our help. *(He repeats the open/ select business)* "And Brutha said to Simony: Where there is darkness we will make a great light. Rely on thy faith for the words of Om will lighten thy darkness and warm thy spirit." *(He kneels, pensive for a moment, then reaches into his pocket and draws out a box of matches. He lights one and moves to apply it to the Book of Om)*

Blackout.

Scene Six
The Vampire's Castle

Thunder crashes and lightning flashes, off; the sound of rain continues.

IGOR *(carrying a cobwebby candlestick)*, NANNY OGG *and* MAGRAT GARLICK *enter.*

IGOR Thorry about crathing on that corner. I'm afraid the wheelth are alwayth falling off. It'th ecthpected, you thee?

NANNY OGG You might have damn' well warned us! We was thrown all over the place!

IGOR The old marthter did thomething to the road back there. Coach wheelth alwayth come off there. The marthter thaid it brought in the vithitorth.

MAGRAT GARLICK It didn't occur to you to mention this?

IGOR Thorry. It'th been a buthy day. Welcome to the de Magpyrth' cathle.

NANNY OGG Well, we're miles from anywhere, the coach is wrecked, it's raining. We couldn't stay out all night, what with the babby an'all. A castle's a castle. It'll have locks. And all the vampires are in Lancre. I don't think the count's going to be very happy with you, though, Igor.

IGOR Thod him. I'm going to pack my thtuff and head for Blintz. Alwayth a job for a good Igor up there. More lightning thriketh per year than anywhere in the mountainth, they thay.

NANNY OGG *(wiping the spit from her eye)* Good job we're soaked already. And Igor: if you haven't been thtraight, sorry straight with us, I'll have your guts for garters.

IGOR Oh, that'th more than a man could pothibly hope for.

IGOR *exits into an interior room.*

NANNY OGG What?

MAGRAT GARLICK *(with a giggle)* Haven't you noticed the looks he's been giving you?

NANNY OGG What him? And I haven't even got me best drawers on!

MAGRAT GARLICK I think he's a bit of a romantic, actually.

NANNY OGG Oh, I don't know, I really don't. I mean, it's flatterin' and everything, but I don't really think I could be goin' out with a man with a limp.

MAGRAT GARLICK Limp what?

NANNY looks surprised at such a comment from MAGRAT.

(pleased with the effect) I am a married woman, you know.

NANNY OGG Yes, of course. And is Verence, you know, all right in the – er—

MAGRAT GARLICK Oh yes, everything's fine. But now I understand what your jokes were about.

NANNY OGG What all of them?

MAGRAT GARLICK Well, not the one about the priest, the old woman and the rhinoceros.

NANNY OGG I should just about hope so! I didn't understand that one until I was forty!

IGOR enters.

IGOR There'th only the thervanth here. You could thtay in my old quarterth in the old tower. There're thick wallth and doorth.

MAGRAT GARLICK Nanny would really like that. She was just saying what good legs you've got.

IGOR Do you want thome? I've got plenty and I could uthe the thpathe in the ithe-houthe. I'm your man, if you need an organ.

MAGRAT splutters quietly. NANNY *seems oblivious – she is, after all, in "crone" mode.*

NANNY OGG   What? You've got bits of people stored in ice? Bits of strange people? Chopped up?

IGOR   No. Not thtrangerth. Family.

NANNY OGG   You chopped up your family?

IGOR   It'th a tradithion. Every Igor leaveth hith body to the family. Why wathte good organth?

MAGRAT GARLICK   But – who does all the cutting and sewing?

IGOR   I do. Dab hand with a needle and thread. Learned it on my father'th knee. Practithed it on me Grandad'th kidneyth.

Suddenly SCRAPS *bounds in. He's a large dog seemingly made up of spare parts from about ten different dogs.*

Thcrapth! Hallo, boy! Have you mithed me? *(He ruffles* SCRAPS*'s ears)*

Thith ith my dog, Thcrapth. He'th a thilly old thing.

NANNY OGG   Scraps. Yes. Good name.

IGOR   He'th theventy-eight yearth old. Thome of him.

MAGRAT GARLICK   Very neat stitching. He looks well on it. Happy as a dog with two... Oh, I see he has got two tails.

IGOR   It'th a thpare. I thought, if he'th happy with one, jutht think of the fun he'll have with two.

NANNY *starts to open her mouth, but* MAGRAT *beats her to it.*

MAGRAT GARLICK   Nanny! Don't even think it! Tails, he was talking about. Not – anything else.

IGOR   Oh, I thought of that ageth ago. It'th obviouth. Thaves on wear and tear. I experimented on mythelf.

There is a pause.

NANNY OGG *(very nonchalantly)* Now – what are we talking about here?

IGOR Heartth.

NANNY OGG Oh hearts. You've got two hearts. Splendid. You're a bit of a self-made man on the quiet, aren't you?

IGOR The old count uthed to like Thcrapth. He uthed to come and pet him every night before he went out. Golden dayth, them wath. I wouldn't give you tuppenth for thith lot. Do you know, they wanted me to get rid of Thcrapth? I saw Lacrimotha kick him onceth. *(A new thought)* Can I get you ladieth anything to eat?

NANNY OGG
MAGRAT GARLICK } *(together; very quickly)* No!

IGOR Thcrapth. Play dead.

SCRAPS *rolls over and plays dead.*

Thee? He rememberth!

MAGRAT GARLICK Won't we be cornered if the de Magpyrs come?

IGOR Oh, they never come down to my quarterth. Not modern enough for them.

MAGRAT GARLICK What about weapons?

IGOR Thtackth of them. The old marthter wath very keen on that. "Igor" he'd thay, "Igor, make thertain the windowth are clean and there'th lotth of lemonth and garlic and tho on around the plathe." Very fair, the old marthter.

NANNY OGG *(kneeling down and tickling* **SCRAP's** *tummy)* But that would mean he'd die, wouldn't it?

IGOR You win thome, you lothe thome. "The day vampireth win all the time," he'd thay, "that'll be the day we get knocked back beyond return." Mind you, he'd get annoyed when people pinched hith thockth. He'd thay: "Thod, that wath thilk. Ten dollarth a pair in Ankh-Morpork."

NANNY OGG *(wiping her eye)* And he probably spent a lot on blotting paper, too. You're a bright chap, aren't you, Igor?

IGOR Yeth. I have a couthin at Untheen Univerthity, you know.

NANNY OGG Really? What's he do there?

IGOR Floatth around in hith jar, mothtly. Thall I thow you the old marthter'th holy water collection?

MAGRAT GARLICK Sorry? A vampire collected holy water?

NANNY OGG I get it. He was a sportsman, right? And a good sportsman always gives the prey a decent chance.

MAGRAT GARLICK I don't follow.

NANNY OGG Being killed's nothing to a vampire. They always finds a way of coming back. If they're not too hard to kill and it's all a bit of an adventure for people, well, like as not they'll just stake him or chuck him in the river and go home. He has a nice restful decade or so and then comes back from the grave. That way, he never gets totally wiped out and the lads of the village get some healthy exercise.

MAGRAT GARLICK But the de Magpyrs will come after us, Nanny. They'll see the crashed coach and they'll find us.

NANNY OGG It'll take them a little while. And we'll have time to get prepared. Now we'll try things my way. I'm not good at thinkin' like Granny Weatherwax, but I'm good at actin' like me. Let's kick some bat.

Blackout.

Scene Seven
The Main Square Of Escrow

Night. Still thunder can be heard, a howling wind, and rain.

VLAD, AGNES, PERDITA *and a couple of other* **VAMPIRES, KRIMSON** *and* **MORBIDIA (TRACY),** *enter.*

VLAD Here we are. This is where we usually meet up. The town square.

AGNES NITT So this is Escrow? But it's charming.

VLAD You're not seeing it at its best, in the dark and after all this rain. Father paid for the town clock there.

AGNES NITT Vampires have a lot of money, do they?

VLAD Well, the family's always owned land and the money mounts up over the centuries. And obviously, we don't enjoy a particularly active social life.

AGNES NITT Or spend much on food.

VLAD Yes, yes, very good.

A bell starts to toll.

Now you'll see. And you'll understand.

AGNES NITT What's the bell for? It's the middle of the night.

VLAD Yes, but it doesn't happen very often and our covenant says never more than twice in a month. You've seen how prosperous the place is.

Townspeople start to enter. Some are still in nightclothes, with shawls or coats over them. They all look downtrodden and without hope. The mayor enters with them, wearing his chain of office over his dressing-gown.

People are safe in Escrow. They've seen reason. No shutters on the windows, see? They don't have to bar their windows or hide in the cellar. They exchanged fear for security. They... *(He staggers slightly)* Sorry. I felt a little – strange. What was I saying?

AGNES NITT You were saying how happy everyone is because the vampires visit, or some such clap-trap.

The **VAMPIRES** *stand on the other side of the stage, observing.*

VLAD Oh yes, yes. Because... *(He pulls a hanky out of his pocket and mops his brow)* because, well, you'll see. Is it rather cold here?

AGNES NITT No.

The **COUNT** *and* **COUNTESS** *enter, with* **LACRIMOSA.** *Another couple of* **VAMPIRES** *also enter.*

COUNT Ah, Miss Nitt.

LACRIMOSA You've still got her? Oh, well—

COUNT I'll just go and have a brief word with the mayor. He appreciates being kept informed. *(He moves to the mayor in the manner of a member of the royal family making an official visit to a factory)*

AGNES NITT Oh, my gods.

VLAD I know what you're thinking. Listen, it could be much worse. It used to be much worse—

The **COUNT** *moves back to* **AGNES** *and* **VLAD.**

COUNT Good news. There are three children who have just turned twelve. We have a little ceremony, before the main lottery. A sort of rite of passage. I think they look forward to it, to tell the truth.

PERDITA He's watching to see how you react. The others are just vicious like Lacrimosa or stupid like Vlad, but this one will go for the throat if you so much as blink at the wrong

time. So don't blink. Even figments of the imagination want
to live...

VLAD It's nothing dramatic. A little drop of blood. Father went
to the school to explain about citizenship...

AGNES NITT *(hoarsely)* How nice. Do they get a badge? And
a certificate?

COUNT No. But what a good idea. Yes. Something to be treasured
in later life. Yes, a badge and a certificate. Splendid. Well,
let us get on. I see the Mayor has assembled the children
in front of the town hall.

PERDITA What's been done to them? They're just standing
around like pigs queuing for Hogswatch!

The **COUNT** *moves towards the Mayor, but* **LACRIMOSA**
blocks his way.

LACRIMOSA Why do you always have to start?

COUNT Lacrimosa! What's got into you? I am the head of the
clan!

LACRIMOSA Oh, really? For ever?

COUNT Well, yes, of course!

LACRIMOSA So we'll be pushed around by you for ever? We'll
just be your children for ever?

COUNT My dear, what do you—?

LACRIMOSA And don't try that voice on me! That only works on
the meat! So I'll be sent to my room for being disobedient
for ever?

COUNT We did let you have your own rack.

LACRIMOSA And for that I have to smile and be nice with
(indicating **AGNES***)* meat?

COUNTESS Don't you dare speak to your father like that!

VLAD And don't talk about Agnes like that!

LACRIMOSA Did I use the word Agnes? I don't believe I did.

COUNT *(slipping into* **WEATHERWAX**-*speak)* I can't be having with all this arguing!

The **COUNT** *and* **COUNTESS** *react momentarily to this unusual turn of phrase.*

LACRIMOSA That's it, isn't it? We don't argue! We just do what you say – forever! Vlad was right!

COUNT *(turning to* **VLAD***)* Indeed? Right about what, pray?

VLAD's *mouth opens and shuts a couple of times as he phrases his reply.*

VLAD I...er... I may have mentioned that the whole Lancre business might be considered unwise...

COUNTESS Oh? You know so much about wisdom all of a sudden and you're barely two hundred?

COUNT Unwise?

LACRIMOSA I'd say stupid! Little badges? Gifts? We don't give anything! We're vampires! We take what we want, like this...

LACRIMOSA *grabs a villager and moves to bite his/her throat. Suddenly, she halts a good foot from the villager's neck and a guttural noise emerges from her throat.*

What – did you do? My throat feels... You did something!

Some of the other **VAMPIRES** *are looking a little queasy, holding their throats, falling to their knees. The villagers look astonished.*

COUNTESS Actually, I don't feel very well either. I did say that wine wasn't a good idea.

COUNT *(staring at* **AGNES NITT***)* It's you, isn't it?

LACRIMOSA Of course it's her! You know that old woman put herself somewhere and she knew Vlad was soppy on that... that...

The action freezes during the following.

PERDITA She's not in here, is she?

AGNES NITT Don't you know?

PERDITA Well, I don't think she is – but is it me doing the thinking?

AGNES NITT Look, she's in that priest, not me!

PERDITA You only thought that because you thought the baby was too obvious.

AGNES NITT *turns to* **LACRIMOSA**. *The action unfreezes.*

AGNES NITT Why don't you crawl back into your coffin and rot, you slimy little maggot!

A strobe light comes on. In slow motion **AGNES NITT** *swings a real haymaker which sends* **LACRIMOSA** *reeling back. The villagers are stunned, but begin to show signs of "life".*

I don't know where Granny Weatherwax went. Maybe she is in here with me, eh? *(She adopts a* "**GRANNY WEATHERWAX**" *voice)* And if you strike me down again I'll bite my way up through your boots!

COUNT *(moving to face* **AGNES NITT***)* Nice try. But I don't think so, Miss Nitt...

Suddenly, the mayor moves forwards. He throws his chain over the **COUNT**'s *head and pulls him to the ground. The villagers break out of their trance. They move forward and start to attack the* **VAMPIRES***. The* **COUNT** *moves some of the junior* **VAMPIRES** *forward to take the crowd's attack.*

The **COUNT, COUNTESS** *and* **LACRIMOSA** *flee.*

VLAD There's no time to waste, Agnes – join us now.

AGNES NITT *(dreamily)* Yes...yes.

PERDITA *(very irate)* NO-O-O-O-O!!!

VLAD *moves to bite* **AGNES**'s *neck.*

Blackout (including the strobe).

Scene Eight
Atop A Mountain

There is the sound of the wind.

GRANNY WEATHERWAX *and* OATS *enter.* OATS *is supporting* GRANNY.

OATS *(out of breath)* Won't be long now.

GRANNY WEATHERWAX *(also very weary)* You don't know that!

OATS No, I was just trying to be cheery.

GRANNY WEATHERWAX Hasn't worked.

OATS I'll go if you want me to.

GRANNY WEATHERWAX Never asked you to come.

OATS You'd be dead if I hadn't!

GRANNY WEATHERWAX That's no business of yours!

OATS My god, Mistress Weatherwax, you try me sorely.

GRANNY WEATHERWAX Your god, Mr Oats, tries everyone. That's what gods does. And they lays down rules all the time. Mostly in your holy book. Let's hear some of his clever words, then.

OATS I – er – I've misplaced it. Must've left it behind when we stopped last time.

GRANNY WEATHERWAX *and* OATS *exchange a look. She knows he burned it to save her. He knows she knows.*

But in his Letter to the Simonites he says it is through other people that we truly become people.

GRANNY WEATHERWAX Good. Well, he got that one right.

OATS And he said we should take light into dark places.

GRANNY *says nothing.*

I thought I'd mention that, because when you were—you know – with the anvil – you said something very similar.

GRANNY WEATHERWAX You listened? Can you remember everything I said?

OATS I think so.

GRANNY WEATHERWAX Can you forget? You wouldn't be so unkind as to pass on the ramblings of a poor ol' woman who was probably off her head, would you?

OATS What ramblings were these, Mistress Weatherwax?

GRANNY WEATHERWAX Well done. *(She pauses)* Shame about your book of holy words. Terrible thing to burn all them words.

OATS The worthwhile ones don't burn.

GRANNY WEATHERWAX You're not too stupid, are you? This Om of yours. Anyone seen him?

OATS It is said three thousand witnessed his manifestation at the Great Temple when he made the Covenant and saved the prophet Brutha from torture and martyrdom.

GRANNY WEATHERWAX I bet now they're arguin' about what was actually seen, though, right?

OATS Well, yes, there are various opinions...

GRANNY WEATHERWAX That's people for you. Now if I'd see him, really alive, it'd be in me like a fever. If I thought there was some god who really did care about people, well, you wouldn't catch me sayin' "There are two sides to every question". Sacrificin' your own life, one day at a time, to the flame, declarin' the truth of it, workin' for it, breathin' the soul of it. That's religion. Anything else is just...bein' nice. Anyway, that's what I'd be if I really believed. But I don't think that's fashionable now, 'cos nowadays if you sees evil, you has to wring your hands and say, "Oh deary me, we must debate this". Don't chase faith, 'cos you'll never catch it. But perhaps you can live faithfully. That's my two-pennorth. *(She shivers)* You got another of them holy books on you?

OATS No.

GRANNY WEATHERWAX A book of hymns? Slim volume of prayers for young people?

OATS No.

GRANNY WEATHERWAX Damn. *(She collapses)*

The wind sounds fade.

Blackout.

Scene Nine
The Town Square In Escrow

There are a couple of unidentified dead vampires on stage. One of the bodies is positioned so that the head is not visible. The mayor also lies dead near the front of the stage.

A group of villagers, including **GERTRUDE** *and* **PIOTR**, *with stakes and hammers, is about to stake* **AGNES**. *She has a lemon in her mouth and is missing one stocking.*

AGNES NITT *(removing the lemon)* Hey, hey, hey, what's going on? Do I look like a vampire? *(Referring to the lemon)* What's this, for goodness' sake? And who took off my left stocking? If it wasn't a woman, there's going to be trouble, I warn you. *(She squirms slightly and looks down her top)* And are these poppy seeds in my bosom? This is a very tasteless display.

GERTRUDE She doesn't act like a vampire! She doesn't look like one, neither.

AGNES NITT *(affronted, despite herself)* Excuse me?

HANS She did fight the other ones.

PIOTR Yeah, but one of them did bite her. *(He points to* **AGNES**'*s neck)*

AGNES NITT *(feeling her neck. She has been bitten, but doesn't want them to know)* Must've been a bad shot in the poor light. I'd – er – I'd kill for a cup of tea, though. And let me shake out some of these poppy seeds. I feel like a wholemeal loaf. *(She indicates the dead vampires)* I see you got some, then.

GERTRUDE Yeah, but they killed the mayor and Mr Vlack.

AGNES NITT The rest got away? *(She points to the vampire body with the concealed head)* Is that one Vlad de Magpyr? The one that bit...tried to bite me?

GERTRUDE We can check. Piotr, show her the head.

PIOTR *reaches offstage and picks up a head which he shows to* **AGNES.**

AGNES NITT No. That's not him.

PERDITA Vlad was taller.

PIOTR *(putting down the head)* They'll be heading back to the castle. On foot. They were running. They didn't seem to be able to fly. What was it you did to them?

AGNES NITT Me?

PIOTR They couldn't even bite us properly.

HANS And they were squabbling like kids when they left. You've got a pointy hat – did you put a spell on them?

AGNES NITT I don't know. I really don't. I may have done.

PIOTR Well, we're going after them. Bring everyone.

The whole cast freezes during the next short exchange.

PERDITA They're going to kill the vampires and let the children watch.

AGNES NITT Good.

PERDITA But it'll give them nightmares!

AGNES NITT No. It'll take the nightmares away. Sometimes, everyone has to know the monster is dead and remember, so that they can tell their grandchildren. They tried to turn people into things. But – vampires don't miss, but Vlad must have done, because I'm not a vampire. I couldn't even eat steak tartare.

PERDITA It's changed you, though.

AGNES NITT How?

PERDITA You're sharper – edgier – nastier.

The cast unfreezes.

AGNES NITT *("aloud")* Maybe it's about time I was, then.

PIOTR Sorry, miss?

AGNES NITT Oh, nothing. Come on then. To the castle. Does
anyone have a spare axe?

Blackout.

Scene Ten
On The Road To The Castle

The stage is lit with moonlight, patterned by tree gobos.
There is the sound of the wind in the trees.

The COUNT, COUNTESS, VLAD *and* LACRIMOSA *enter.*
They seem a little out of breath. CRYPTOPHER *and*
MORBIDIA *(and others?) follow them on.*

COUNTESS We'll burn that ungrateful place to the ground!

LACRIMOSA *Afterwards* we'll burn that place to the ground.
This is what kindness leads to, Father.

COUNTESS After you paid for that belltower, too.

COUNT Burn the village? Yes, that might be a good idea. We
would have to make sure that word got around, though.

LACRIMOSA You think *this* news won't get round?

COUNT It'll be dawn soon, Lacci. Because of my training, you
will regard it as rather a nuisance, not a reason to crumble
to dust. Reflect on this.

LACRIMOSA That Weatherwax woman did this, didn't she?
She's put herself somewhere and she's attacking us. It can't
be in the baby. What about Agnes, Vlad? Plenty of room
in there. Vlad?

VLAD *(vaguely)* Mmm...?

LACRIMOSA I saw you give in and bite her. So romantic. They'll
have to use a long stake to hit any vital organ.

COUNT She'd have put it somewhere close. It stands to reason.
It must have been someone in the hall.

COUNTESS One of the other witches, surely?

COUNT I wonder.

LACRIMOSA That stupid priest.

COUNT That would appeal to her.

VLAD Not Igor?

COUNT I wouldn't give that a moment's thought.

LACRIMOSA What about Agnes then? She was there when it all went wrong in Escrow.

VLAD At least I bit someone. What was wrong with you?

COUNTESS Yes, Lacci, you were acting very strangely.

LACRIMOSA If she was hiding in me, I'd know!

COUNT I wonder. She just has to find a weak spot.

LACRIMOSA Father, she's a witch. Honestly, we're acting as if she's got some sort of terrible power.

COUNT Perhaps it was Vlad's Agnes after all. *(He stares at* VLAD*)*

COUNTESS We're nearly at the castle. We'll all feel better for an early day.

LACRIMOSA Our best coffins got taken to Lancre. Someone was so sure of himself!

COUNT Don't you adopt that tone with me, young woman!

LACRIMOSA I'm two hundred years old. Pardon me, but I think I can choose any tone I like.

COUNTESS That's no way to speak to your father!

LACRIMOSA Really, Mother, you might act as though you had two brain cells of your own.

COUNTESS It is not your father's fault that everything's gone wrong!

COUNT Everything has not gone wrong. It's just a temporary setback!

LACRIMOSA It won't be when the Escrow cattle tell their friends. Come on, Vlad, back me up here.

COUNT And if they tell them, what can they do? Oh, there'll be a bit of protesting, but the survivors will see reason. In the meantime, we have those witches waiting for us – with the baby.

LACRIMOSA And we've got to be polite to them, I suppose?

COUNT Oh, I don't think we need go that far. Let them live, perhaps...

IGOR *and* NANNY *appear on the castle ramparts.*

IGOR *throws a (holy) water bomb; it lands on or by* CRYPTOPHER, *showering him. He reacts as though struck with acid, writhing in agony.*

IGOR That'th water from the Holy Turtle Pond of Thquintth. Blethed by the Bithop himthelf. You won't get patht uth, thuckerth! The cathtle doorth are firmly bolted!

CRYPTOPHER *continues to writhe in agony.*

COUNT Really, Cryptopher. It's all in the mind you know.

COUNTESS Aren't you going to do something?

COUNT Oh, very well. *(He gestures)*

CRYPTOPHER *falls dead to the ground.*

You know that should not have happened. He was obviously not – truly one of us.

IGOR *throws another water bomb, which lands near the* COUNT. *Despite himself, he winces with pain as the water hits him.*

Some error appears to have crept in.

Now it's the COUNTESS*'s turn to fall into* WEATHERWAX-*speak.*

COUNTESS I've never been one to put myself forward. Nobody could call me an interferin' old busybody, but I strongly suggest you find a new plan, dear. One which works, perhaps? *(She looks slightly confused at the rather rustic turn of phrasing she has found herself using)*

The COUNT *might give the* COUNTESS *a look.*

COUNT   At least we can still control the weather. They won't keep me out of my own castle. This will shift them. *(He gestures again)*

There is a flash of lightning, a crash of thunder, and an explosion near NANNY *and* IGOR *and another at the castle door.*

Come on!

The VAMPIRES *exit into the castle, through the onstage curtains.*

The lights go out at stage level.

NANNY OGG   Well, that was easy, I don't think.

IGOR   Didn't I menthion they can control the weather? *(He sniffs)* What'th that thmell?

NANNY OGG   Your boots are on fire!

IGOR   Damn. And thethe feet were nearly new thicth month ago. Old Mikhailth parentth thaid I could have them when that tree fell on him coth I'd given him a thpare arm a few yearth back after he had that accident with a thircular thaw.

NANNY OGG   Blimey! People round here don't so much die as pass on.

IGOR   What goeth around, cometh around.

The lights cross-fade to the castle interior.

The VAMPIRES *storm in.*

LACRIMOSA   Well, at least we've managed to walk through our own front door. Well done. And your new plan is?

COUNT We'll kill everyone.

LACRIMOSA What everyone? All at once?

COUNT Oh, you can save some for later if you must.

COUNTESS *(clutching his arm)* Oh, this does remind me of
our honeymoon. Such romance – and we met such lovely
people, too. Do you remember Mr and Mrs Harker?

COUNT Very fondly. I recall they lasted nearly all week. Now,
listen all of you. Holy symbols will not hurt us. Cryptopher
just was not concentrating. Garlic is just another member
of the allium family. Do onions hurt us? Are we frightened
of shallots? No. We've just got a bit tired, that's all. *(He rubs
his head. Again, he drifts into* WEATHERWAX-*speak)* I can't
be havin' with this at all...

The others look at the COUNT.

What?

COUNTESS Are you all right, dear? She couldn't have got into
your head, could she?

COUNT Me? No. I've had hundreds of years of experience. No
village witch could get past my defences. *(He clears his
throat)* My throat, mind you, is parched. Do we have any
– tea?

COUNTESS What is tea?

COUNT It – grows on a bush, I think.

COUNTESS How do you bite it, then?

COUNT You – lower it into boiling water, I believe...

LACRIMOSA While it's still alive?

COUNT *(drifting off into a reverie)* Sweet biscuits....

COUNTESS I think you should try to get a grip, dear.

LACRIMOSA This – tea. Is it brown?

COUNT Yes.

LACRIMOSA Because when we were in Escrow I was going to
bite one of the cattle and I had this horrible mental picture
of a cup full of the wretched stuff.

COUNT I don't know what's happening to me. So let's stick to
what we do know, shall we? Obey our blood. There's no
need to panic. Careful thought will save us. That is why
we survive.

LACRIMOSA It's not working! I'm a vampire! I'm supposed
to crave blood! And all I can think about is a cup of tea
with three sugars in it, whatever the hell that is! That old
woman's got something to do with it, can't you see?

COUNT Not possible. Oh, she's sharp for a human – *(again,
without being aware of it, he suddenly adopts* GRANNY
WEATHERWAX'*s mode of speech)* but I don't reckon there's
any way she could get into your head, or mine.

LACRIMOSA *(talking like* GRANNY WEATHERWAX *but without
noticing)* You're even talkin' like her!

COUNT Be resolute. Remember, that which does not kill us can
only make us stronger.

LACRIMOSA And that which does kill us leaves us dead! That
water hurt you!

COUNT A momentary lapse of concentration. That old witch
is not a threat. She's a vampire. Subservient to us. I am
supremely confident.

LACRIMOSA What have you done to us? You taught us to see
religious symbols as just patterns and lines, but there are
patterns everywhere – window frames, carriage wheels,
flagstones. I see holy symbols everywhere! You've taught
us to see these patterns – but now they hurt!

COUNTESS It'll be dawn soon. Will it hurt?

COUNT It won't! Of course it won't! It's a learned psycho-
chromatic reaction! It's all in the mind!

VLAD What else is in our mind, Father?

COUNT Nothing' s in our minds that we didn't put there! I saw
that old witch's mind! It's weak. She relies on trickery! She
couldn't possibly find a way in!

COUNTESS Well, I think we're all getting a little bit over-excited.
I think we should all settle down and have a nice cup of...
A nice...of tea... A cup of....

They all drift off into a tea-inspired reverie.

LACRIMOSA *(breaking the mood, shouting)* We're vampires!!!

COUNT *(bellowing)* Then let's act like them!!!

The COUNT *storms out. The others follow.*

Blackout.

Scene Eleven
The Road To The Vampire's Castle

An exterior, night-time scene. Thunder crashes.

A section of broken door, with knocker attached, lies on the stage.

OATS *enters, carrying* **GRANNY WEATHERWAX**. **OATS** *is singing a hymn.*

OATS *(singing)*
"...BURN WITH A CLEAR BRIGHT LIGHT, AND OM'S GREAT NAME BE PRAISED..."
(speaking) It's quite amazing how much heavier you seem, Mistress Weatherwax.

GRANNY WEATHERWAX *(muttering, "recalling" the things the* **COUNT** *has been saying)* ...kill them all...frightened of shallots...saw that old witch's mind...can't be havin' with all this... *(She comes to)* Are we here then?

OATS Yes.

GRANNY WEATHERWAX What happened to your holy amulet?

OATS It got lost.

GRANNY WEATHERWAX Put me down, would you?

OATS What's the magic word?

GRANNY WEATHERWAX Oh, I don't think a holy man like you should be having with magic words. But the holy words are: "Do What I Tell You or Get Smitten".

OATS *puts* **GRANNY WEATHERWAX** *down.*

There is a male scream, off.

Not a female. I reckon the girls have started. Let's give them a hand, shall we?

They move to the door.

Ah, yes. I'd definitely say that, given the splintered remains of the vampire's front door, the girls are definitely here. Right, you're the gods-botherer, so you'd better knock.

OATS Knock? But there's no door!

GRANNY WEATHERWAX We wouldn't want to sneak in, now, would we? You're a good man, Mr Oats? Even without your holy book and your amulet?

OATS Er – I try to be.

GRANNY WEATHERWAX Well, this is where you find out. This is where we both find out.

OATS *picks up the piece of the door bearing the knocker and knocks.*

The lights come up on the balcony – the castle battlements.

A moment's pause, then a **VAMPIRE** *enters, running.*

VAMPIRE Tea! I must have tea!

The **VAMPIRE** *crosses the stage and exits, still running.*

NANNY *and* **IGOR** *enter on the balcony. They are carrying hammers, stakes, and a net bag of lemons.* **NANNY** *stops and leans against a parapet to catch her breath.*

NANNY OGG Excitin', isn't it? *(She listens a moment)* Granny's here somewhere. Don't ask me how I know, I just do. That vampire was craving tea, and only Esme can mess someone's head up like that. I'd like to see the bloodsucker who could put one over on her.

IGOR I wouldn't.

OATS *knocks again and* **NANNY** *leans over and sees* **GRANNY WEATHERWAX** *and* **OATS.**

NANNY OGG I knew it! Coo-ee, Esme!

GRANNY WEATHERWAX Is the baby all right?

NANNY OGG Magrat and young Esme are safely locked up in the crypt. Strong door.

IGOR And Thcrapth ith guarding them.

NANNY OGG This is Igor. A man of many parts.

GRANNY WEATHERWAX So I see.

NANNY OGG Why'd you bring old Soapy Sam?

GRANNY WEATHERWAX Couldn't seem to shake him off.

NANNY OGG We bin despatchin' vampires like no-ones business, Esme. It's really easy. They're hardly even fightin' back. (*She points, off*) Look, there's a crowd comin'. And Agnes is leading them.

AGNES NITT, *followed by a crowd of villagers, enters and marches up to the door by* **GRANNY** *and* **OATS.**

AGNES NITT I can't be havin' with this! I can't think straight. It's you, isn't it?

GRANNY WEATHERWAX One of them bit you, yes?

AGNES NITT Yes! And somehow you spoke to me!

GRANNY WEATHERWAX No. Not me. I reckon that was just something in your blood talking. Who're all these people?

AGNES NITT They're from Escrow, it's a town not far away... The de Magpyrs treated them like – well – farm animals.

GRANNY WEATHERWAX The count's still here. We're not goin' until we've dealt with the count.

OATS Excuse me, but where did you say the queen was?

NANNY OGG In the crypt. Safe as houses.

OATS So, these vampires can't turn themselves into mist, then, and sneak through keyholes?

GRANNY WEATHERWAX (*to* IGOR) Can they?

IGOR Oh, the old count would never do anything like that!

NANNY OGG Yes, but he played fair!

There is the sound of barking, off. It is **SCRAPS**.

IGOR *(heading for the exit)* That wath Thcrapth! Quick!

   IGOR *exits.*

AGNES NITT Thcrapth?

GRANNY WEATHERWAX Come on! Agnes – you get the vampires and help Nanny. Mr Oats, you and me are goin' to find the kitchen.

OATS The kitchen?

GRANNY WEATHERWAX At a time like this, we could all do with a nice cup of tea.

They all exit into the castle.

Blackout.

Scene Twelve
The Crypt

The noise of fighting comes from offstage.

MAGRAT, **SCRAPS** *and the baby are on stage.* **MAGRAT**
has a teddy bear with her.

NANNY OGG *(offstage)* Magrat? It's all right, dear, we've got them
all. Even the count. You can open the door now. Er... Lawks.

MAGRAT GARLICK Is that really you, Nanny?

NANNY OGG *(offstage)* That's right, dear.

SCRAPS *growls.*

MAGRAT GARLICK *(aside, to* **SCRAPS***)* I know, boy. I know.
*(Aloud, to "***NANNY***")* Thank goodness. Just tell me that joke
about the old woman, the priest and the rhinoceros and I'll
let you in, then.

NANNY OGG *(offstage)* Er, I don't think we've got time for that,
dear.

MAGRAT GARLICK *(laughing)* Nice try! I'm not as stupid as
that, Count de Magpyr!

COUNT *(offstage)* I'd hoped you would be sensible about this.
Ah, well...

There is an explosion and the **COUNT** *bursts in.*

MAGRAT GARLICK Stay back! Come near me and you'll get
this! *(She waves a teddy bear at the* **COUNT***)*

COUNT *(taking the teddy bear from her and tossing it away)* I
don't think that will work. Even if you sharpened it! Where
is the countess? I thought she might be able to persuade
you to listen to reason.

MAGRAT GARLICK *(brandishing a jar of mist at the* **COUNT***)*
Not in a jar she can't! Oh dear, you mean that smoke that

came through my keyhole was her? I caught her in this. *(She turns the jar round and we see the label: "Garlic")* I do hope the garlic doesn't hurt her too much!

COUNT You killed her! You little fiend. However, she'll be back. Your pesky dog won't be so lucky.

The COUNT *kills* SCRAPS.

Come!

The COUNT *drags* MAGRAT *offstage.*

A moment, then NANNY *and* IGOR *enter.*

IGOR *(immediately dropping to* SCRAPS*'s side)* Thcrapth! Thcrapth! They've killed him! The barthtardth!

NANNY OGG They've got Magrat and the babby!

IGOR He wath my only friend.

NANNY OGG *(lifting* IGOR *by his collar, apparently effortlessly)* Listen, you're going to have one very serious enemy really soon, my lad, unless you help us out right now! Oh for heavens' sake... *(She pulls a hanky out of her knicker leg and hands it to him)* Blow!

IGOR *trumpets into the hanky.*

Now, where would they take them?

AGNES NITT *enters.*

They've got them.

IGOR *(sobbing)* He wath alwayth ready with a waggy tail and hith cold nothe...

NANNY OGG Where, Igor?

IGOR *(not listening)* That'th it. I've put up with it too long. I'm going to get thomeone who will thort them out!

IGOR *bustles off.*

NANNY OGG I reckon they're still in the castle. But why are they staying? Why haven't they run away?

AGNES NITT Granny wouldn't run.

NANNY OGG No, Granny likes a showdown. And they're thinkin' like her. Somehow she's makin' them think like her...

AGNES NITT She thinks like her, too!

NANNY OGG Let's hope she's had more practice, then. Come on.

They exit.

Blackout.

Scene Thirteen
Elsewhere In The Castle

The COUNT, COUNTESS, LACRIMOSA, VLAD *and a couple of other* VAMPIRES *enter, with* MAGRAT *and the baby. The* COUNT *has the baby in his arms and has hold of* MAGRAT'*s wrist.*

LACRIMOSA *(as she enters)* Thank goodness we don't take after your side of the family, that's what I say.

VLAD This is ridiculous. Why are we still here? We've got the child! There're plenty of other castles.

COUNT That would be running away.

VLAD *(rubbing his forehead)* And surviving.

LACRIMOSA Father's right. We don't run.

Some of the crowd enter; NANNY OGG *is among them. One is carrying a wooden slop bucket which will be important later.*

COUNT Step back, please.

The crowd does so.

Well done. Absolute obedience, just like playing chess. If you have the queen, you've as good as won. It doesn't matter if a few pawns are lost.

VLAD That's a nasty way to talk about Mother.

COUNT I am very attached to your mother. And she will find a way to return. In the meantime, the rest will do her good...

NANNY OGG *shoulders her way through the crowd.*

Ah, the inestimable Mrs Ogg.

NANNY OGG Don't you go smarmin' me! I'm fed up with you smarming at me smarmily as if you was Mr Smarm! Now you just free the both of them, or—

COUNT Ah, so quickly we get to "or". But I will say: you will all leave the castle and then we shall see. Perhaps we shall let the queen go. But the little princess – isn't she charming? She can remain as our guest.

MAGRAT GARLICK *(squirming ineffectively in the* COUNT*'s grasp)* She's coming back to Lancre with us, you bastard!

COUNT That's very bad language for a queen. Struggle all you like; I am very strong, even for a vampire. But you're right, we shall all go back to Lancre...

We are aware of a noise over the speakers as of someone stirring a nice cup of tea. It builds to a crescendo during the following.

One big happy family, living in the castle. Don't blame yourself for your failure, Mrs Ogg, I'm sure others will do that for you...

The crowd parts.

The recorded noise stops and is replaced by the actual sound of GRANNY*'s stirring.*

GRANNY WEATHERWAX *enters and strolls in, stirring a cup of tea.*

GRANNY WEATHERWAX No milk in this place. Not to be wondered at, really. I sliced a bit of lemon, but it's not the same, I always think. *(She puts the spoon in the saucer with a metallic clink)* Am I too late? *(She looks around at the crowd)* I'm an old lady. I'd like to sit down, thank you so much.

One of the crowd brings forward a stool. GRANNY WEATHERWAX *sits.*

Sorry, count, what were you saying?

COUNT Ah, Esmerelda, at last you come to join us. The call of the blood is too strong to disobey, yes?

GRANNY WEATHERWAX I certainly hope so.

COUNT We are all walking out of here, Granny Weatherwax.

> GRANNY WEATHERWAX *stirs her tea. The* VAMPIRES *become transfixed by this. During the following, she keeps moving as if to drink her tea, but stops at the last moment. Each time, the* VAMPIRES *eye the brew longingly.*

You're not leaving here.

You have no choice but to obey me. You know that.

GRANNY WEATHERWAX Oh, there's always a choice.

COUNT *(looking at her fixedly)* No. You couldn't have resisted. Not even you.

GRANNY WEATHERWAX *(still stirring)* Oh, I won't say it didn't cost me.

COUNT *(looking to the others for support)* We do have the queen and the baby. I believe you think highly of them.

GRANNY WEATHERWAX *(raising the cup to her lips, but not drinking)* Kill 'em. It won't benefit you.

NANNY OGG
MAGRAT GARLICK } *(together)* Granny!

PERDITA I know what she did.

AGNES NITT So do I.

GRANNY WEATHERWAX *(to* NANNY *and* MAGRAT*)* He's bluffing.

LACRIMOSA Oh? You'd like a vampire queen one day, would you?

GRANNY WEATHERWAX Had one once, in Lancre. Griminir the Impaler, she was. Never laid a tooth on anyone.

LACRIMOSA The Impaler?

GRANNY WEATHERWAX Didn't say she was a nice person, just said she wasn't a bloodsucker. She drew the line at drinking blood. You could do that, too.

LACRIMOSA You know nothing about true vampires!

GRANNY WEATHERWAX I know more'n you'd think. And I know
about Nanny Ogg. She likes a drink. She'll tell you it has
to be best brandy – and that's certainly what she desires.
But really she'll settle for beer like everyone else. But you
wouldn't settle for black puddings, would you, because what
you drink is power over people. I know you like I know
myself. And one of the things I know is that you ain't goin'
to harm a hair on that baby's head. If'n it had any. Which
it will. You can't, see. *(She picks up the cup, scrapes it on
the saucer and goes as if to drink. She pauses)* So all I'm
really here for is to see if you get justice or mercy. It's just
a matter of choosing.

LACRIMOSA You think we won't harm meat? Watch! *(She crosses
to the baby and swings her arm round in a vicious blow
which stops short of the baby as if it had hit a force field)*

GRANNY WEATHERWAX *(putting the cup back on the saucer)*
Can't do it.

LACRIMOSA I nearly broke my arm!

GRANNY WEATHERWAX *(picking up the cup and moving as if
to drink)* Shame.

COUNT You've put something magical in the child, haven't you?

GRANNY WEATHERWAX *(putting the cup back again)* Can't
imagine who'd think I'd do such a thing. So here's my offer,
you see. You hand back Magrat and the baby and we'll
chop your heads off. *(She picks up the cup and moves as if
to drink from it)*

COUNT And that's what you call justice, is it?

GRANNY WEATHERWAX *(putting the cup down)* No, that's what
I call mercy.

COUNT *(bellowing)* For goodness' sake, woman, are you going
to drink that damn tea or not?

GRANNY WEATHERWAX *(sipping the tea and pulling a face)* Why, what have I been thinking of? I've been so busy talking, it's gone cold. *(She turns and pours the tea into the nearby slopbucket)*

LACRIMOSA *groans.*

It'll probably wear off soon, but until it does, you see, you'll not harm a child, you'll not harm Magrat, you hate the thought of drinking blood and you won't run because you never run from a challenge.

VLAD What will wear off?

GRANNY WEATHERWAX They're strong, your walls of thought. I couldn't get through 'em. So I didn't. You wanted to know where I'd put myself. It didn't go anywhere. I just put it in something alive, and you took it. You invited me in. I'm in every muscle in your body and I'm in your head, oh yes – I was in the blood, count. In the blood. You've been Weatherwaxed. All of you. You all drank my blood. You didn't vampire me. I Weatherwaxed you. And you always obey your blood, don't you?

IGOR *bursts in.*

IGOR Right! Now we'll thort you out! I've brought him back!

Lightning flashes and thunder crashes. Smoke billows out.

The curtains part and in walks the **OLD COUNT**, *a Bela Lugosi-type* **VAMPIRE**.

OLD COUNT Good morning.

NANNY OGG Another bloody vampire?

IGOR *(moving to* **NANNY OGG**) Not juht any vampire! It'th the old marthter! Old Red Eyeth ith Back!

GRANNY WEATHERWAX *(moving towards the* **COUNT**) I know all about what you can and can't do. Because you let me in.

And that means you can't do what I can't do. You think just
like me, but I've been doin' it longer and I'm better at it!

COUNT You're meat! Clever meat!

GRANNY WEATHERWAX And you invited me in. I'm not the
sort to go where I'm not welcome, I'm sure.

COUNT How sure are you that I won't harm this child?

GRANNY WEATHERWAX I wouldn't. So you can't.

The **COUNT** *wrestles with his feelings.*

COUNT It could have worked.

AGNES NITT You mean it could have worked for you!

COUNT We are vampires. We cannot help what we are!

GRANNY WEATHERWAX Only animals can't help what they are.
Will you give the child, now?

COUNT If I...? No! I don't have to bargain! I can fight you.
Just as you fought me! If I walk out of here, I don't think
anyone here will dare to stop me. Look at you, all of you.
Now look at me. And now, look at him *(He indicates the*
OLD COUNT*)* Is that what you want?

GRANNY WEATHERWAX Sorry? Oh, you mean the "Old Master".
The old Count de Magpyr, I believe?

OLD COUNT Your servant, ma'am.

GRANNY WEATHERWAX I doubt it.

PIOTR Oh no one minded him. He only ever came around every
few years and anyway if you remembered about the garlic
he wasn't a problem.

OLD COUNT *(moving across to* **PIOTR***)* You look familiar. One
of the Ravi family, aren't you?

PIOTR Piotr, sir. Son of Hans.

OLD COUNT Ah yes. Very similar bone structure. Do remember
me to your grandmother.

PIOTR She passed away ten years ago, sir.

OLD COUNT Really? I'm so sorry. Time passes so quickly when you're dead. A very fine figure in a nightdress, as I recall.

HANS Yes, he was all right. We got a nip every now and then, but we got over it.

OLD COUNT That's a familiar voice. Are you a Veyzen?

HANS Yes sir.

OLD COUNT Related to Arno Veyzen?

HANS Great-granddaddy, sir.

OLD COUNT Good man. Killed me stone dead seventy-five years ago. Stake right through the heart at twenty paces. You should be proud.

HANS We still got the stake hung over the fireplace, y'honour.

OLD COUNT Splendid! Good to see the old ways being kept up...

COUNT You can't possibly prefer that! He's a monster!

AGNES NITT But he never made an appointment! I bet he never thought it was all an arrangement!!!

COUNT (*edging towards the door*) No, this is not how it is going to happen. If you think I won't harm my charming hostages, then try to stop me. Does anyone really believe that old woman?

OATS *enters, carrying the double-headed axe.*

OATS Have you ever thought of letting Om into your life?

COUNT Oh...you again. If I can resist her, little boy, you are not a problem.

OATS (*holding out the axe in front of him*) Begone, foul fiend...

COUNT (*pushing the axe aside*) Oh dear me. You stupid little man with your stupid little faith in your stupid little god?

OATS It lets me see things as they are!

COUNT Really? And you think you can stand in my way? *(He points at the axe)* That isn't even a religious symbol.

OATS *(looking momentarily crestfallen)* Oh. *(He smiles)* Let's make it so.

The strobe light comes on. **OATS** *pulls back the axe and swings it in a large arc, "severing" the* **COUNT**'s *head. The* **COUNT** *grasps his throat and, for the rest of the scene, clasps at his head as if to stop it from falling off. The other* **VAMPIRES** *now cower back against the walls. The strobe light goes off.*

GRANNY WEATHERWAX If I has a fault, it's not knowing when to turn and run. Who says there's no mercy in the world? Someone'll take you down to a nice coffin and I daresay fifty years will just fly by and maybe you'll wake up with more sense.

The crowd do not like this.

They want you deader than that, see? And there's ways, oh yes. We could burn you to ashes and scatter them in the sea.

A murmur of approval from the crowd.

Or throw' em up in the air in the middle of a gale. Don't reckon you'd ever pull yourself together after that.

There is another murmur of approval from the crowd.

But, no, fifty years is long enough to think about things. People need vampires. Helps them remember what stakes and garlic are for. Come on – two of you take him down to the vaults. Show some respect for the dead.

PIOTR That's not enough! Not after he—

GRANNY WEATHERWAX Then when he comes back, deal with him yourself. Teach your children! Don't trust the cannibal just 'cos he's usin' a knife and fork. Remember that vampires don't go where they're not invited. This time round it's up to me. My choice. You tried to take my mind away. And that's everything to me. Reflect on that. Try to learn. Take him away.

The COUNT *is led out.*

GRANNY *turns to the* OLD COUNT.

So – you're the old master, eh?

OLD COUNT Alison Weatherwax? I have a good memory for necks.

GRANNY WEATHERWAX What? No! How do you know the name?

OLD COUNT Why she passed through here – what, fifty years ago or more. We met briefly and then she cut off my head and stuck a stake in my heart. A very spirited woman. You're a relative, I suppose?

GRANNY WEATHERWAX Granddaughter.

OLD COUNT Everything was so much simpler then. But now, apparently, we're in modern times...

GRANNY WEATHERWAX That's what they say.

OLD COUNT I do apologise for my nephew. Quite out of keeping for a vampire. Would you people from Escrow like to kill these ones, too? It's the least I could do.

VLAD *(to* AGNES NITT*)* You wouldn't let them kill me, would you? We could have... We might... You wouldn't, would you?

AGNES NITT *takes* VLAD*'s hand.*

PERDITA I suppose we could work on him.

AGNES NITT Vlad. I'd even hold their coats.

GRANNY WEATHERWAX Yes, very nice but it ain't happenin'. Take 'em away count. Teach 'em the old ways.

OLD COUNT Thank you, ma' am. You are a wise woman, Granny Weatherwax, for someone who has yet to live even a single lifetime. Goodbye.

The **VAMPIRES** *and the villagers withdraw, separately.*

PERDITA Why didn't Granny let the villagers kill them? Death's too good for them!

AGNES NITT That's why she didn't let them have it.

OATS *(moving downstage centre)* I killed him.

AGNES NITT Sort of. Hard to tell with vampires.

OATS There was nothing else to do! Everything just went—

AGNES NITT I don't think anyone's complaining.

PERDITA You've got to admit he's rather attractive. If he lost the boil.

MAGRAT GARLICK You were very brave.

OATS No I wasn't. I thought Mistress Weatherwax was going to do something.

MAGRAT GARLICK She did. Oh, she did. What will you do, Igor?

IGOR Thtay on, of courthe. The old marthter had loth of ideath while he wath dead. He thinkth we ought to build a funfair. I've got to go and work on thome ideath.

AGNES NITT We're very sorry about Scraps. Perhaps we can find you a puppy?

IGOR Thankth, but no. There'th only one Thcrapth.

IGOR *exits.*

GRANNY WEATHERWAX I want to go home now. I just want to sleep for a week. I'm dyin' for a cuppa.

AGNES NITT You should have drunk the one you made. You had us all slavering for it!

GRANNY WEATHERWAX Where would I get tea round here? It was just mud in water. But I know Nanny keeps a bag on her person. Make the tea, Magrat.

AGNES NITT *is about to protest, but* **MAGRAT** *gives her the baby.*

MAGRAT GARLICK Certainly, Granny. I'll just see where Igor keeps his kettle.

Suddenly **VERENCE** *bursts on, followed by* **JASON** *and* **SHAWN OGG**.

VERENCE Right! Don't worry, ladies, we'll save you! Right – where are they?

MAGRAT GARLICK Verence... Verence, dear...?

VERENCE Take my kingdom, would they...? Er, what is it, dear?

MAGRAT GARLICK Granny's sorted it, dear. Come and help me make the tea.

VERENCE Oh. Right.

MAGRAT *and* **VERENCE** *exit.*

NANNY OGG And you two can help me to clean up this castle. There's bits of vampire everywhere.

JASON OGG ⎱
SHAWN OGG ⎰ *(together)* Yes. Mum.

NANNY OGG, JASON OGG, SHAWN OGG, AGNES NITT *and* **PERDITA** *leave.*

A pause.

OATS I felt your hands on the axe, Mistress Weatherwax. When I, when we killed the count. *(Pause)*

No reaction.

It looks like it's going to be a fine day.

GRANNY WEATHERWAX There's a storm comin' down from the Hub later.

OATS Well...at least that'll be good for the crops, then. *(He beams, suddenly happy)* I feel blessed to have been here.

GRANNY WEATHERWAX Really? I generally feels that way about the sunrise. You would too, at my time o' life. *(Mostly to herself)* She never went to the bad, then, whatever people said. And you'd have to be on your toes, with that old count. She never went to the bad. You heard him say it, mm? He didn't have to.

OATS Er, yes.

GRANNY WEATHERWAX She'd have been older than me, too. Bloody good witch was Nana Alison. Sharp as a knife. Had her funny little ways, but then, who hasn't?

OATS No one I know, certainly.

GRANNY WEATHERWAX *(snapping out of it)* Right. You're right.

OATS I, er, feel I should thank you.

GRANNY WEATHERWAX For helping you across the mountains, you mean?

OATS Erm. I see the world differently now. Everywhere I look I see something holy. *(He looks at* **GRANNY WEATHERWAX***)*

For the first time, **GRANNY WEATHERWAX** *smiles properly. There is a pause.*

GRANNY WEATHERWAX That's a good start, then. Got a pencil on you, Mr Oats?

OATS *hands* **GRANNY WEATHERWAX** *a pencil.*

Thank you. See how that tea's coming, would you?

OATS *nods and exits.*

GRANNY *takes out her "I ATE'NT DEAD" card and starts to write on it.*

The lights cross-fade to the Mad Scientist's Laboratory.

Thunder rumbles. On stage is a table with **SCRAPS***'s body on it, covered by a black cloth.*

IGOR *enters.*

IGOR *pulls back the black cloth to reveal* SCRAPS*'s body. He moves to one side of the stage and pulls a huge "Frankenstein" switch. There is a flash of lightning and a flash pod goes off on stage.* SCRAPS *twitches back to life.*

IGOR Thcrapth! *(He hugs* SCRAPS*)*

The lights cross-fade again to GRANNY WEATHERWAX. *She closes her eyes. The lights change from full stage coverage to a single spot.* GRANNY WEATHERWAX *slowly turns her card to face front. It now reads: "I STILL ATE'NT DEAD".*

Blackout.

FURNITURE AND PROPERTY LIST

ACT I

Handkerchief (in **Vlad**'s pocket)
Invitation (in **Count**'s pocket)
Igor: half a potato
Reception guests: glasses of wine
Shawn Ogg: tray of glasses of wine
Oats: Book of Om
Royal crib and baby
The Expert: card reading "I ATE'NT DEAD"
Nanny Ogg: pointy stick
Piece of paper (in **Oats**'s hat)
Oats: drink
Igor: large boxes
Table
Chairs
Three sets of knives, forks, spoons, cups
Boiled sweet (in **Nanny Ogg**'s pocket)
Agnes Nitt: Granny's heavily-gilded invitation
Bell rope
Lacrimosa: four wine glasses
Vlad: bottle of red wine, corkscrew
Cards with religious symbols on them (in **Count**'s pocket)
Oats: iron poker
Oats: large boxes and bags, fluffy bunny
Bridge made of stone slab
Magrat Garlick: glass ball
Granny Weatherwax: card saying "GOE AWAY"
Apple
Water bottle
Sandwich
Granny Weatherwax's box
Cauldron
Agnes Nitt: tea things
Candle in holder
Igor: grubby bucket

Bottle of holy water (in **Agnes Nitt**'s pocket)
Corporal Svitz: crossbow
Piece of card, lemon (in **Nanny Ogg**'s pocket)

ACT II

Bed
Oats: glass of water
Oats: anvil
Double-headed axe
Oats: cup of tea, biscuit
Oats: hammer, stake
Box of matches (in **Oats**'s pocket)
Agnes Nitt: lemon
Piotr: head
Igor: holy water bomb
Section of broken door with knocker attached
Nanny and **Igor:** hammers, stakes, net bag of lemons
Magrat Garlick: teddy bear
Jar of mist labelled "Garlic" (in Magrat Garlick's pocket)
Handkerchief (in **Nanny Ogg**'s knicker leg)
Villager: wooden slop bucket
Pencil (in **Oats**'s pocket)
Huge "Frankenstein" switch

LIGHTING PLOT

Practical fittings required: candle, "glowing" anvil
Various interior and exterior scenes

ACT I

To open: Darkness; house lights up

Cue 1	When ready *Fade house lights; bring up eerie light* *on stage.*	(Page 1)
Cue 2	Fog swirls across the stage *Lightning.*	(Page 1)
Cue 3	The **Magpyrs** snarl and turn us *Blackout.*	(Page 2)
Cue 4	**The Expert** enters *Bring up follow spot on* **The Expert.**	(Page 2)
Cue 5	**The Expert:** "...anything can happen." *Bring up light on the vampires.*	(Page 2)
Cue 6	**The Expert:** "...some elderly hunchback..." *Bring up spot on* **Igor.**	(Page 3)

Cue 7	**The Expert:** "...daughter's naming
	   ceremony."
	Cut lights on vampires and **Igor;**
	   bring up spot on **Agnes Nitt.**
		(Page 3)

Cue 8	**The Expert:** "She took over as third
	   witch—"
	Cross-fade to spot on **Magrat Garlick,**
	   upstage left.
		(Page 4)

Cue 9	**The Expert:** "...but you know it's true." *Cut spot on* **Magrat.**	(Page 4)
Cue 10	**The Expert:** "Let's get on with our play, shall we?" *Blackout.*	(Page 5)

Cue 11   When ready   (Page 6)
         Bring up exterior lights.

Cue 12   The **de Magpyrs** exit   (Page 9)
         Blackout.

Cue 13   When ready   (Page 10)
         Bring up general interior lighting.

Cue 14   **Shawn Ogg** scuttles over to **Verence**   (Page 13)
         Cross-fade lights to balcony.

Cue 15   **The Expert** enters   (Page 15)
         Bring up spot on **Expert**.

Cue 16   **The Expert** holds up the card   (Page 16)
         Cut spotlight.

Cue 17   **Magrat Garlick:** "You'll have to wait
         and see."   (Page 16)
         *Cross-fade lights back to general
         interior setting.*

Cue 18   Onstage curtains open   (Page 20)
         *Bring up interior lights on cottage
         setting.*

Cue 19   **Granny Weatherwax:** "...do without me!"   (Page 20)
         Cut lights on cottage setting.

Cue 20   **Verence:** "Count, can I present—"   (Page 27)
         Flash of lightning.

Cue 21   **Vlad:** "We shall meet again, Agnes Nitt." (Page 29)
         Blackout.

Cue 22   When ready   (Page 30)
         Bring up lights on dim, "night" setting.

Cue 23   **Nanny Ogg:** "Come on."   (Page 32)
         Blackout.

Cue 24   When ready   (Page 33)
         Bring up general interior lighting.

Cue 25   The vampires laugh   (Page 37)
Blackout.

Cue 26   When ready   (Page 38)
Bring up general interior lighting.

Cue 27   All exit hurriedly   (Page 45)
Blackout.

Cue 28   When ready   (Page 46)
Bring up exterior lighting; "dawn"
setting, with window-frame gobo.

Cue 29   **Countess:** "Do join us in a light meal."   (Page 51)
Blackout.

Cue 30   When ready   (Page 52)
Bring up general exterior lighting.

Cue 31   **Agnes Nitt:** "Her mind's wandering!"   (Page 55)
Blackout.

Cue 32   When ready   (Page 56)
Bring up lights on balcony.

Cue 33   **Count:** "So very predictable."   (Page 56)
Blackout.

Cue 34   When ready   (Page 57)
Bring up general interior lighting.

Cue 35   All exit   (Page 61)
Blackout.

Cue 36   When ready   (Page 62)
Bring up lights on balcony.

Cue 37   **Count:** "...all in the past now."   (Page 62)
Blackout.

Cue 38   When ready   (Page 63)
Bring up dim general exterior lighting.

Cue 39   **Magrat Garlick:** "There's no path."   (Page 64)
Strobe light.

Cue 40 Trickling sound of babbling brook
        comes up   (Page 66)
        Cut strobe light; bring up tight
        spotlight on **Witches**.

Cue 41 **Nanny Ogg** points   (Page 67)
        Flash.

Cue 42 Onstage curtains open   (Page 67)
        Cross-fade lights to cave setting behind
        curtains.

Cue 43 **Nanny Ogg, Agnes Nitt** et al move
        away from the cave   (Page 69)
        Cross-fade lights downstage.

Cue 44 **Agnes Nitt:** "Listen!"   (Page 70)
        Cross-fade lights to cave.

Cue 45 **Nanny Ogg** moves back to the others (Page 71)
        Cross-fade lights downstage.

Cue 46 **Nanny Ogg:** "Back to my place, I think." (Page 72)
        Blackout.

Cue 47 When ready   (Page 73)
        Bring up general interior lighting.

Cue 48 The **Witches** head us with the table (Page 77)
        Blackout.

Cue 49 When ready   (Page 78)
        Bring up general interior lighting
        with covering spot on candle.

Cue 50 **Oats** sighs and returns to his book (Page 78)
        Blackout.

Cue 51 When ready   (Page 79)
        Bring up general interior lighting.

Cue 52 The **Witches** exit   (Page 84)
        Blackout.

Cue 53	When ready *Bring up general exterior lighting.*	(Page 85)
Cue 54	**Jason Ogg:** "I s'pose." *Blackout.*	(Page 86)
Cue 55	When ready *Bring up general interior lighting.*	(Page 87)
Cue 56	**Count**: "...you could harm us?" *Flash of lightning.*	(Page 87)
Cue 57	**Granny** makes a small gesture *Lights flicker.*	(Page 90)
Cue 58	**Granny** gestures again *Lights flicker.*	(Page 91)
Cue 59	The **de Magpyrs** stare at the audience *Blackout.*	(Page 97)

ACT II

To open: General interior lighting

Cue 60	**Granny Weatherwax** kneels by the anvil *Strobe light.*	(Page 100)
Cue 61	Eerie noise begins *Anvil glows.*	(Page 100)
Cue 62	**Granny Weatherwax:** "You don't scare me no more!" *Blackout.*	(Page 103)
Cue 63	When ready *Bring up general interior lighting.*	(Page 104)
Cue 64	**Perdita:** "And perhaps a pin." *Blackout.*	(Page 107)
Cue 65	When ready *Bring up general interior lighting; lightning on exterior backing.*	(Page 108)

Cue 66   **Granny Weatherwax** and **Oats**
      move off   (Page 113)
      Blackout.

Cue 67   When ready   (Page 114)
      Bring up general exterior lighting.

Cue 68   They all head for the exit   (Page 115)
      Blackout.

Cue 69   When ready   (Page 116)
      Bring up general exterior lighting plus
         lightning effect.

Cue 70   **Oats** moves to apply the match to the
      Book of Om   (Page 119)
      Blackout.

Cue 71   When ready   (Page 120)
      Bring up general interior lighting with
         lightning effect on exterior backing.

Cue 72   **Nanny Ogg:** "Let's kick some bat." (Page 124)
      Blackout.

Cue 73   When ready   (Page 125)
      Bring up general exterior lights;
         night effect.

Cue 74   **Agnes Nitt:** "...you slimy little maggot!" (Page 129)
      Strobe light.

Cue 75   **Vlad** moves to bite **Agnes**   (Page 130)
      Blackout including strobe.

Cue 76   When ready   (Page 131)
      Bring up general exterior lighting.

Cue 77   **Granny Weatherwax** collapses   (Page 133)
      Blackout.

Cue 78   When ready   (Page 134)
      Bring up general exterior lighting.

Cue 79 **Agnes Nitt:** "Does anyone have
            a spare axe?"   (Page 136)
          Blackout.

Cue 80 When ready   (Page 137)
          Bring up general exterior lighting;
          moonlight with tree gobos.

Cue 81 The **Count** gestures   (Page 140)
          Lightning.

Cue 82 The vampires exit into the castle   (Page 140)
          Cut lights at stage level.

Cue 83 **Igor:** "What goeth around,
            cometh around."   (Page 140)
          Cross-fade lights to the castle interior.

Cue 84 The **Count** storms out. The others
            follow   (Page 143)
          Blackout.

Cue 85 When ready   (Page 144)
          Bring up general exterior lighting;
          night effect.

Cue 86 **Oats** knocks with the knocker   (Page 145)
          Bring up lights on balcony.

Cue 87 All exit into the castle   (Page 147)
          Blackout.

Cue 88 When ready   (Page 148)
          Bring up general interior lighting.

Cue 89 All exit   (Page 150)
          Blackout.

Cue 90 When ready   (Page 151)
          Bring up general interior lighting.

Cue 91 **Igor:** "I've brought him back!"   (Page 155)
          Lightning.

Cue 92   **Oats:** "Let's make it so."   (Page 158)
           Strobe light on.

Cue 93   The vampires cower against the walls   (Page 158)
           Strobe light off.

Cue 94   **Granny** starts to write on the card   (Page 162)
           Cross-fade lights to Mad Scientist's
           Laboratory.

Cue 95   **Igor** pulls the switch   (Page 163)
           Flash of lightning.

Cue 96   **Igor** hugs Scraps   (Page 163)
           Cross-fade lights to
           Granny Weatherwax.

Cue 97   **Granny Weatherwax** closes her eyes   (Page 163)
           Change lights from full stage coverage
           to spot on **Granny Weatherwax.**

Cue 98   **Granny Weatherwax** turns her card
           to face front   (Page 163)
           Blackout.

EFFECTS PLOT

ACT I

Cue 1   House lights dim   (Page 1)
            Menacing music; fog; rumbles of
            thunder.

Cue 2   The **de Magpyrs** advance   (Page 2)
            Music swells.

Cue 3   As Scene Two begins   (Page 6)
            Coach and horses approach and stop.

Cue 4   **Verence:** "Count, can I present—"
            Flash of lightning   (Page 27)
            Rumble of thunder.

Cue 5   **Countess:** "...could not have come,
            of course."   (Page 28)
            Band strikes up.

Cue 6   **Vlad:** "We shall meet again, Agnes Nitt." (Page 29)
            Cut music.

Cue 7   As Scene Six begins   (Page 30)
            Owl hoots; wind soughs in trees; fade
            as scene proceeds.

Cue 8   **Nanny Ogg** throws a boiled sweet
            off stage   (Page 39)
            Clatter of magpie's cry.

Cue 9   **Nanny Ogg** sees something in the
            cottage   (Page 41)
            Magpie cries.

Cue 10   **Agnes** exits. Slight pause   (Page 42)
            Tree rustles.

Cue 11   **Agnes Nitt:** "Give me a moment,
            will you?"   (Page 42)
            Sound of cloth ripping.

Cue 12	**Agnes Nitt:** "Got it!" *Sound of wood breaking.*	(Page 42)
Cue 13	**Agnes Nitt:** "Aah!" *Thump.*	(Page 42)
Cue 14	**Agnes**: "...cushioned my fall." *Magpie cries.*	(Page 43)
Cue 15	**Oats:** "Does that count?" *Wolf howls.*	(Page 45)
Cue 16	As Scene Eleven begins *Flapping wings and cries of magpies;* *fade as scene proceeds.*	(Page 56)
Cue 17	Establish **Count** on balcony **Count**'s *recorded dialogue as script* *p. 56.*	(Page 56)
Cue 18	As Scene Fourteen begins *Wind (continuing) and mist/smoke.*	(Page 63)
Cue 19	Strobe light comes on *Wind gets louder; more mist/smoke.*	(Page 64)
Cue 20	**Agnes Nitt:** "...that little stream by now?" *Sound of large rushing river.*	(Page 65)
Cue 21	**Nanny Ogg:** "Yes? And?" *Fade river sound, bring up trickling* *of babbling brook; fade this as scene* *progresses.*	(Page 66)
Cue 22	**Nanny Ogg:** "There!" She points *Flash; loud noise.*	(Page 67)
Cue 23	The witches move to **Granny Weatherwax** *Fade wind; bring up dripping water* *sound.*	(Page 69)

Cue 24   The witches move away from
          Granny Weatherwax   (Page 69)
          *Fade dripping water sound; bring
          up wind.*

Cue 25   Lights cross-fade to the cave   (Page 70)
          *Fade wind; bring up dripping water
          sound.*

Cue 26   **Nanny Ogg** moves back to **Agnes**
          and **Magrat**   (Page 71)
          *Fade dripping water sound; bring up
          wind.*

Cue 27   **Nanny Ogg:** "Back to my place, I think." (Page 72)
          Fade wind sounds.

Cue 28   As Scene Sixteen begins   (Page 78)
          Wind; then **Oats**'s *recorded dialogue
          as p. 78.*

Cue 29   **Oats** returns to his book   (Page 78)
          Fade wind sounds.

Cue 30   Flash of lightning   (Page 87)
          Crash of thunder.

Cue 31   **Granny Weatherwax:** "I'd call
          that unambitious."   (Page 91)
          Loud and bright explosion.

ACT II

Cue 32   **Granny Weatherwax** holds the anvil   (Page 100)
          *Crackling sound; eerie sound,
          continuing throughout scene.*

Cue 33   Second **Granny Weatherwax** enters   (Page 102)
          Recorded dialogue as pp. 102–103.

Cue 34   **Granny Weatherwax:** "You don't
          scare me no more!"   (Page 103)
          Cut eerie sound.

Cue 35 As Scene Three opens   (Page 108)
          Thunder.

Cue 36 As Scene Four opens   (Page 114)
          Wind.

Cue 37 They all head for the exit   (Page 115)
          Fade wind sounds.

Cue 38 As Scene Five opens   (Page 116)
          Thunder; heavy rain; continuous
          through this scene and the next two.

Cue 39 As Scene Six opens   (Page 120)
          Thunder.

Cue 40 As Scene Seven begins   (Page 125)
          Mix in sound of howling wind.

Cue 41 **Vlad**: "Yes, yes, very good."   (Page 125)
          Bell tolls.

Cue 42 **Vlad** moves to bite **Agnes**'s neck   (Page 130)
          Fade all weather sounds except the
          wind.

Cue 43 **Granny Weatherwax** *collapses*   (Page 133)
          Fade wind sounds.

Cue 44 As Scene Ten begins   (Page 137)
          Wind in trees.

Cue 45 Lightning   (Page 140)
          Thunder; explosions near **Nanny**
          and castle door.

Cue 46 As Scene Eleven begins   (Page 144)
          Thunder.

Cue 47 **Count** *(offstage)*: "Ah, well..."   (Page 148)
          Explosion.

Cue 48   **Count**: "...we shall all go back to
            Lancre ..."   (Page 152)
            *Noise of someone stirring a cup of
            tea; builds to crescendo as scene
            progresses.*

Cue 49   **Igor:** "I've brought him back."   (Page 155)
            Thunder; smoke.

Cue 50   The lights cross-fade to the laboratory   (Page 162)
            Thunder.

Cue 51   Flash of lightning   (Page 105)
            Flash pod goes off on stage.